Internet Gambling Prohibition Act of 1999

INTERNET GAMBLING PROHIBITION ACT OF 1999

HEARING

BEFORE THE

SUBCOMMITTEE ON CRIME

OF THE

COMMITTEE ON THE JUDICIARY
HOUSE OF REPRESENTATIVES

ONE HUNDRED SIXTH CONGRESS

SECOND SESSION

ON

H.R. 3125

MARCH 9, 2000

Serial No. 102

COMMITTEE ON THE JUDICIARY

HENRY J. HYDE, Illinois, *Chairman*

F. JAMES SENSENBRENNER, JR., Wisconsin
BILL McCOLLUM, Florida
GEORGE W. GEKAS, Pennsylvania
HOWARD COBLE, North Carolina
LAMAR S. SMITH, Texas
ELTON GALLEGLY, California
CHARLES T. CANADY, Florida
BOB GOODLATTE, Virginia
STEVE CHABOT, Ohio
BOB BARR, Georgia
WILLIAM L. JENKINS, Tennessee
ASA HUTCHINSON, Arkansas
EDWARD A. PEASE, Indiana
CHRIS CANNON, Utah
JAMES E. ROGAN, California
LINDSEY O. GRAHAM, South Carolina
MARY BONO, California
SPENCER BACHUS, Alabama
JOE SCARBOROUGH, Florida
DAVID VITTER, Louisiana

JOHN CONYERS, JR., Michigan
BARNEY FRANK, Massachusetts
HOWARD L. BERMAN, California
RICK BOUCHER, Virginia
JERROLD NADLER, New York
ROBERT C. SCOTT, Virginia
MELVIN L. WATT, North Carolina
ZOE LOFGREN, California
SHEILA JACKSON LEE, Texas
MAXINE WATERS, California
MARTIN T. MEEHAN, Massachusetts
WILLIAM D. DELAHUNT, Massachusetts
ROBERT WEXLER, Florida
STEVEN R. ROTHMAN, New Jersey
TAMMY BALDWIN, Wisconsin
ANTHONY D. WEINER, New York

THOMAS E. MOONEY, SR., *General Counsel-Chief of Staff*
JULIAN EPSTEIN, *Minority Chief Counsel and Staff Director*

SUBCOMMITTEE ON CRIME

BILL McCOLLUM, Florida, *Chairman*

STEVE CHABOT, Ohio
BOB BARR, Georgia
GEORGE W. GEKAS, Pennsylvania
HOWARD COBLE, North Carolina
LAMAR S. SMITH, Texas
CHARLES T. CANADY, Florida
ASA HUTCHINSON, Arkansas

ROBERT C. SCOTT, Virginia
MARTIN T. MEEHAN, Massachusetts
STEVEN R. ROTHMAN, New Jersey
ANTHONY D. WEINER, New York
SHEILA JACKSON LEE, Texas

GLENN R. SCHMITT, *Chief Counsel*
DANIEL J. BRYANT, *Chief Counsel*
RICK FILKINS, *Counsel*
CARL THORSEN, *Counsel*
BOBBY VASSAR, *Minority Counsel*

CONTENTS

HEARING DATE

TEXT OF BILL

OPENING STATEMENT

WITNESSES

LETTERS, STATEMENTS, ETC., SUBMITTED FOR THE HEARING

APPENDIX

INTERNET GAMBLING PROHIBITION ACT OF 1999

THURSDAY, MARCH 9, 2000

HOUSE OF REPRESENTATIVES,
SUBCOMMITTEE ON CRIME,
COMMITTEE ON THE JUDICIARY,
Washington, DC.

The subcommittee met, pursuant to notice, at 2:09 p.m., in Room 2138, Rayburn House Office Building, Hon. Steve Chabot, presiding.

Present: Representatives Steve Chabot, George W. Gekas, Howard Coble, Robert C. Scott, Anthony D. Weiner, and Sheila Jackson Lee.

Staff Present: Daniel J. Bryant, chief counsel; Glenn R. Schmitt, chief counsel; Carl Thorsen, counsel; Veronica Eligan, staff assistant; and Bobby Vassar, minority counsel.

OPENING STATEMENT OF PRESIDING CHAIRMAN CHABOT

Mr. CHABOT. We are going to come to order. Good afternoon. I would like to welcome everyone to this afternoon's hearing on behalf of myself and on behalf of Chairman McCollum, who is not able to be here today. We will be hearing from three panels of witnesses on the Internet Gambling Prohibition Act of 1999, introduced by Representatives Goodlatte and LoBiondo.

In the 105th Congress, the subcommittee held two hearings on this issue and legislation and subsequently approved similar legislation by voice vote. In the 106th Congress, Representatives Goodlatte and LoBiondo have again introduced legislation that is very similar to the bill that passed the U.S. Senate by unanimous consent late last year.

H.R. 3125 was favorably reported to the full Judiciary Committee on November 3, 1999. Since that subcommittee markup, ranking members Conyers and Scott wrote to Chairman Hyde requesting another hearing on this legislation. This hearing will be the third held on this matter since legislation was introduced to ban Internet gambling in the 105th Congress.

[The bill, H.R. 3125, follows:]

106TH CONGRESS
1ST SESSION

H. R. 3125

To prohibit Internet gambling, and for other purposes.

IN THE HOUSE OF REPRESENTATIVES

OCTOBER 21, 1999

Mr. GOODLATTE (for himself, Mr. LOBIONDO, Mr. WOLF, Mr. BOUCHER, Mr. GIBBONS, and Mr. GOODE) introduced the following bill; which was referred to the Committee on the Judiciary

---

A BILL

To prohibit Internet gambling, and for other purposes.

Be it enacted by the Senate and House of Representatives of the United States of America in Congress assembled,

SECTION 1. SHORT TITLE.

This Act may be cited as the "Internet Gambling Prohibition Act of 1999".

SEC. 2. PROHIBITION ON INTERNET GAMBLING.

(a) IN GENERAL.—Chapter 50 of title 18, United States Code, is amended by adding at the end the following:

"§ 1085. Internet gambling

"(a) DEFINITIONS.—In this section the following definitions apply:

"(1) BETS OR WAGERS.—The term 'bets or wagers'—

"(A) means the staking or risking by any person of something of value other than in a de minimis amount upon the outcome of a contest of others, a sporting event, or a game predominantly subject to chance, upon an agreement or understanding that the person or another person will receive something of greater value than the amount staked or risked in the event of a certain outcome;

"(B) includes the purchase of a chance or opportunity to win a lottery or other prize (which opportunity to win is predominantly subject to chance);

"(C) includes any scheme of a type described in section 3702 of title 28; and

"(D) does not include—

"(i) a bona fide business transaction governed by the securities laws (as that term is defined in section 3(a)(47) of the Securities Exchange Act of 1934 (15 U.S.C. 78c(a)(47))) for the purchase or sale at a future date of securities (as that term is defined in section 3(a)(10) of the Securities Exchange Act of 1934 (15 U.S.C. 78c(a)(10)));

"(ii) a transaction on or subject to the rules of a contract market designated pursuant to section 5 of the Commodity Exchange Act (7 U.S.C. 7);

"(iii) a contract of indemnity or guarantee;

"(iv) a contract for life, health, or accident insurance; or

"(v) participation in a simulation sports game or an educational game or contest that—

"(I) is not dependent solely on the outcome of any single sporting event or nonparticipant's singular individual performance in any single sporting event;

"(II) has an outcome that reflects the relative knowledge and skill of the participants; and

"(III) offers a prize or award to a participant that is established in advance of the game or contest and is not determined by the number of participants or the amount of any fees paid by those participants.

"(2) CLOSED-LOOP SUBSCRIBER-BASED SERVICE.—The term 'closed-loop subscriber-based service' means any information service or system that uses—

"(A) a device or combination of devices—

"(i) expressly authorized and operated in accordance with the laws of a State, exclusively for placing, receiving, or otherwise making a bet or wager described in subsection (f)(1)(B); and

"(ii) by which a person located within any State must subscribe and be registered with the provider of the wagering service by name, address, and appropriate billing information to be authorized to place, receive, or otherwise make a bet or wager, and must be physically located within that State in order to be authorized to do so;

"(B) an effective customer verification and age verification system, expressly authorized and operated in accordance with the laws of the State in which it is located, to ensure that all applicable Federal and State legal and regulatory requirements for lawful gambling are met; and

"(C) appropriate data security standards to prevent unauthorized access by any person who has not subscribed or who is a minor.

"(3) FOREIGN JURISDICTION.—The term 'foreign jurisdiction' means a jurisdiction of a foreign country or political subdivision thereof.

"(4) GAMBLING BUSINESS.—The term 'gambling business' means—

"(A) a business that is conducted at a gambling establishment, or that—

"(i) involves—

"(I) the placing, receiving, or otherwise making of bets or wagers; or

"(II) the offering to engage in the placing, receiving, or otherwise making of bets or wagers;

"(ii) involves 1 or more persons who conduct, finance, manage, supervise, direct, or own all or part of such business; and

"(iii) has been or remains in substantially continuous operation for a period in excess of 10 days or has a gross revenue of $2,000 or more from such business during any 24-hour period; and

"(B) any soliciting agent of a business described in subparagraph (A).

"(5) INFORMATION ASSISTING IN THE PLACING OF A BET OR WAGER.—The term 'information assisting in the placing of a bet or wager'—

"(A) means information that is intended by the sender or recipient to be used by a person engaged in the business of betting or wagering to place, receive, or otherwise make a bet or wager; and

"(B) does not include—

"(i) information concerning parimutuel pools that is exchanged exclusively between or among 1 or more racetracks or other parimutuel wagering facilities licensed by the State or approved by the foreign jurisdiction in which the facility is located, and 1 or more parimutuel wagering facilities licensed by the State or approved by the foreign jurisdiction in which the facility is located, if that information is used only to conduct common pool parimutuel pooling under applicable law;

"(ii) information exchanged exclusively between or among 1 or more racetracks or other parimutuel wagering facilities licensed by the State or approved by the foreign jurisdiction in which the facility is located, and a support service located in another State or foreign jurisdiction, if the information is used only for processing bets or wagers made with that facility under applicable law;

"(iii) information exchanged exclusively between or among 1 or more wagering facilities that are licensed and regulated by the State in which each facility is located, and any support service, wherever located, if the information is used only for the pooling or processing of bets or wagers made by or with the facility or facilities under each State's applicable law;

"(iv) any news reporting or analysis of wagering activity, including odds, racing or event results, race and event schedules, or categories of wagering; or

"(v) any posting or reporting of any educational information on how to make a bet or wager or the nature of betting or wagering.

"(6) INTERACTIVE COMPUTER SERVICE.—The term 'interactive computer service' means any information service, system, or access software provider that operates in, or uses a channel or instrumentality of, interstate or foreign commerce to provide or enable access by multiple users to a computer server, including specifically a service or system that provides access to the Internet.

"(7) INTERACTIVE COMPUTER SERVICE PROVIDER.—The term 'interactive computer service provider' means any person that provides an interactive computer service, to the extent that such person offers or provides such service.

"(8) INTERNET.—The term 'Internet' means the international computer network of both Federal and non-Federal interoperable packet switched data networks.

"(9) PERSON.—The term 'person' means any individual, association, partnership, joint venture, corporation (or any affiliate of a corporation), State or political subdivision thereof, department, agency, or instrumentality of a State or political subdivision thereof, or any other government, organization, or entity (including any governmental entity (as defined in section 3701(2) of title 28)).

"(10) PRIVATE NETWORK.—The term 'private network' means a communications channel or channels, including voice or computer data transmission facilities, that use either—

"(A) private dedicated lines; or

"(B) the public communications infrastructure, if the infrastructure is secured by means of the appropriate private communications technology to prevent unauthorized access.

"(11) STATE.—The term 'State' means a State of the United States, the District of Columbia, the Commonwealth of Puerto Rico, or a commonwealth, territory, or possession of the United States.

"(12) SUBSCRIBER.—The term 'subscriber'—

"(A) means any person with a business relationship with the interactive computer service provider through which such person receives access to the system, service, or network of that provider, even if no formal subscription agreement exists; and

"(B) includes registrants, students who are granted access to a university system or network, and employees or contractors who are granted access to the system or network of their employer.

"(b) INTERNET GAMBLING.—

"(1) PROHIBITION.—Subject to subsection (f), it shall be unlawful for a person engaged in a gambling business knowingly to use the Internet or any other interactive computer service—

"(A) to place, receive, or otherwise make a bet or wager; or

"(B) to send, receive, or invite information assisting in the placing of a bet or wager.

"(2) PENALTIES.—A person engaged in a gambling business who violates this section shall be—

"(A) fined in an amount equal to not more than the greater of—

"(i) the total amount that such person bet or wagered, or placed, received, or accepted in bets or wagers, as a result of engaging in that business in violation of this section; or

"(ii) $20,000;

"(B) imprisoned not more than 4 years; or

"(C) both.

"(3) PERMANENT INJUNCTIONS.—Upon conviction of a person under this section, the court may enter a permanent injunction enjoining such person from placing, receiving, or otherwise making bets or wagers or sending, receiving, or inviting information assisting in the placing of bets or wagers.

"(c) CIVIL REMEDIES.—

"(1) JURISDICTION.—The district courts of the United States shall have original and exclusive jurisdiction to prevent and restrain violations of this section by issuing appropriate orders in accordance with this section, regardless of whether a prosecution has been initiated under this section.

"(2) PROCEEDINGS.—

"(A) INSTITUTION BY FEDERAL GOVERNMENT.—

"(i) IN GENERAL.—The United States may institute proceedings under this subsection to prevent or restrain a violation of this section.

"(ii) RELIEF.—Upon application of the United States under this subparagraph, the district court may enter a temporary restraining order or an injunction against any person to prevent or restrain a violation of this section if the court determines, after notice and an opportunity for a hearing, that there is a substantial probability that such violation has occurred or will occur.

"(B) INSTITUTION BY STATE ATTORNEY GENERAL.—

"(i) IN GENERAL.—The attorney general of a State (or other appropriate State official) in which a violation of this section allegedly has occurred or will occur, after providing written notice to the United States, may institute proceedings under this subsection to prevent or restrain the violation.

"(ii) RELIEF.—Upon application of the attorney general (or other appropriate State official) of an affected State under this subparagraph, the district court may enter a temporary restraining order or an injunction against any person to prevent or restrain a violation of this section if the court determines, after notice and an opportunity for a hearing, that there is a substantial probability that such violation has occurred or will occur.

"(C) INDIAN LANDS.—Notwithstanding subparagraphs (A) and (B), for a violation that is alleged to have occurred, or may occur, on Indian lands (as that term is defined in section 4 of the Indian Gaming Regulatory Act (25 U.S.C. 2703))—

"(i) the United States shall have the enforcement authority provided under subparagraph (A); and

"(ii) the enforcement authorities specified in an applicable Tribal-State compact negotiated under section 11 of the Indian Gaming Regulatory Act (25 U.S.C. 2710) shall be carried out in accordance with that compact.

"(D) EXPIRATION.—Any temporary restraining order or preliminary injunction entered pursuant to subparagraph (A) or (B) shall expire if, and as soon as, the United States, or the attorney general (or other appropriate State official) of the State, as applicable, notifies the court that issued the order or injunction that the United States or the State, as applicable, will not seek a permanent injunction.

"(3) EXPEDITED PROCEEDINGS.—

"(A) IN GENERAL.—In addition to any proceeding under paragraph (2), a district court may, in exigent circumstances, enter a temporary restraining order against a person alleged to be in violation of this section upon application of the United States under paragraph (2)(A), or the attorney general (or other appropriate State official) of an affected State under paragraph (2)(B), without notice and the opportunity for a hearing as provided in rule 65(b) of the Federal Rules of Civil Procedure (except as provided in subsection (d)(3)), if the United States or the State, as applicable, demonstrates that there is probable cause to believe that the use of the Internet or other interactive computer service at issue violates this section.

"(B) HEARINGS.—A hearing requested concerning an order entered under this paragraph shall be held at the earliest practicable time.

"(d) INTERACTIVE COMPUTER SERVICE PROVIDERS.—

"(1) IMMUNITY FROM LIABILITY FOR USE BY ANOTHER.—

"(A) IN GENERAL.—An interactive computer service provider described in subparagraph (B) shall not be liable, under this section or any other provision of Federal or State law prohibiting or regulating gambling or gambling-related activities, for the use of its facilities or services by another person to engage in Internet gambling activity that violates such law—

"(i) arising out of any transmitting, routing, or providing of connections for gambling-related material or activity (including intermediate and temporary storage in the course of such transmitting, routing, or providing connections) by the provider, if—

"(I) the material or activity was initiated by or at the direction of a person other than the provider;

"(II) the transmitting, routing, or providing of connections is carried out through an automatic process without selection of the material or activity by the provider;

"(III) the provider does not select the recipients of the material or activity, except as an automatic response to the request of another person; and

"(IV) the material or activity is transmitted through the system or network of the provider without modification of its content; or

"(ii) arising out of any gambling-related material or activity at an online site residing on a computer server owned, controlled, or operated by or for the provider, or arising out of referring or linking users to an online location containing such material or activity, if the material or activity was initiated by or at the direction of a person other than the provider, unless the provider fails to take expeditiously, with respect to the particular material or activity at issue, the actions described in paragraph (2)(A) following the receipt by the provider of a notice described in paragraph (2)(B).

"(B) ELIGIBILITY.—An interactive computer service provider is described in this subparagraph only if the provider—

"(i) maintains and implements a written or electronic policy that requires the provider to terminate the account of a subscriber of its system or network expeditiously following the receipt by the provider of a notice described in paragraph (2)(B) alleging that such subscriber has violated or is violating this section; and "(ii) with respect to the particular material or activity at issue, has not knowingly permitted its computer server to be used to engage in activity that the provider knows is prohibited by this section, with the specific intent that such server be used for such purpose.

"(2) NOTICE TO INTERACTIVE COMPUTER SERVICE PROVIDERS.—

"(A) IN GENERAL.—If an interactive computer service provider receives from a Federal or State law enforcement agency, acting within its authority and jurisdiction, a written or electronic notice described in subparagraph (B), that a particular online site residing on a computer server owned, controlled, or operated by or for the provider is being used by another person to violate this section, the provider shall expeditiously—

"(i) remove or disable access to the material or activity residing at that online site that allegedly violates this section; or

"(ii) in any case in which the provider does not control the site at which the subject material or activity resides, the provider, through any agent of the provider designated in accordance with section 512(c)(2) of title 17, or other responsible identified employee or contractor—

"(I) notify the Federal or State law enforcement agency that the provider is not the proper recipient of such notice; and

"(II) upon receipt of a subpoena, cooperate with the Federal or State law enforcement agency in identifying the person or persons who control the site.

"(B) NOTICE.—A notice is described in this subparagraph only if it—

"(i) identifies the material or activity that allegedly violates this section, and alleges that such material or activity violates this section;

"(ii) provides information reasonably sufficient to permit the provider to locate (and, as appropriate, in a notice issued pursuant to paragraph (3)(A) to block access to) the material or activity;

"(iii) is supplied to any agent of a provider designated in accordance with section 512(c)(2) of title 17, if information regarding such designation is readily available to the public;

"(iv) provides information that is reasonably sufficient to permit the provider to contact the law enforcement agency that issued the notice, including the name of the law enforcement agency, and the name and telephone number of an individual to contact at the law enforcement agency (and, if available, the electronic mail address of that individual); and

"(v) declares under penalties of perjury that the person submitting the notice is an official of the law enforcement agency described in clause (iv).

"(3) INJUNCTIVE RELIEF.—

"(A) IN GENERAL.—The United States, or a State law enforcement agency acting within its authority and jurisdiction, may, not less than 24 hours following the issuance to an interactive computer service provider of a notice described in paragraph (2)(B), in a civil action, obtain a temporary restraining order, or an injunction to prevent the use of the interactive computer service by another person in violation of this section.

"(B) LIMITATIONS.—Notwithstanding any other provision of this section, in the case of any application for a temporary restraining order or an injunction against an interactive computer service provider described in paragraph (1)(B) to prevent a violation of this section—

"(i) arising out of activity described in paragraph (1)(A)(i), the injunctive relief is limited to—

"(I) an order restraining the provider from providing access to an identified subscriber of the system or network of the interactive computer service provider, if the court determines that there is probable cause to believe that such subscriber is using that access to violate this section (or to engage with another person in a communication that violates this section), by terminating the specified account of that subscriber; and

"(II) an order restraining the provider from providing access, by taking reasonable steps specified in the order to block access, to a specific, identified, foreign online location;

"(ii) arising out of activity described in paragraph (1)(A)(ii), the injunctive relief is limited to—

"(I) the orders described in clause (i)(I);

"(II) an order restraining the provider from providing access to the material or activity that violates this section at a particular online site residing on a computer server operated or controlled by the provider; and

"(III) such other injunctive remedies as the court considers necessary to prevent or restrain access to specified material or activity that is prohibited by this section at a particular online location residing on a computer server operated or controlled by the provider, that are the least burdensome to the provider among the forms of relief that are comparably effective for that purpose.

"(C) CONSIDERATIONS.—The court, in determining appropriate injunctive relief under this paragraph, shall consider—

"(i) whether such an injunction, either alone or in combination with other such injunctions issued, and currently operative, against the same provider would significantly (and, in the case of relief under subparagraph (B)(ii), taking into account, among other factors, the conduct of the provider, unreasonably) burden either the provider or the operation of the system or network of the provider;

"(ii) whether implementation of such an injunction would be technically feasible and effective, and would not materially interfere with access to lawful material at other online locations;

"(iii) whether other less burdensome and comparably effective means of preventing or restraining access to the illegal material or activity are available; and

"(iv) the magnitude of the harm likely to be suffered by the community through the accessibility of illegal activity.

"(D) NOTICE AND EX PARTE ORDERS.—Injunctive relief under this paragraph shall not be available without notice to the service provider and an opportunity for such provider to appear before the court, except for orders ensuring the preservation of evidence or other orders having no material adverse effect on the operation of the communications network of the service provider.

"(4) ADVERTISING OR PROMOTION OF NON-INTERNET GAMBLING.—

"(A) DEFINITIONS.—In this paragraph:

"(i) CONDUCTED.—With respect to a gambling activity, that activity is 'conducted' in a State if the State is the State in which the gambling establishment (as defined in section 1081) that offers the gambling activity being advertised or promoted is physically located.

"(ii) NON-INTERNET GAMBLING ACTIVITY.—The term 'non-Internet gambling activity' means—

"(I) a gambling activity in which the placing of the bet or wager is not conducted by the Internet; or

"(II) a gambling activity to which the prohibitions of this section do not apply.

"(B) IMMUNITY FROM LIABILITY FOR USE BY ANOTHER.—

"(i) IN GENERAL.—An interactive computer service provider described in clause (ii) shall not be liable, under any provision of Federal or State law prohibiting or regulating gambling or gambling-related activities, or under any State law prohibiting or regulating advertising and promotional activities, for—

"(I) content, provided by another person, that advertises or promotes non-Internet gambling activity that violates such law (unless the provider is engaged in the business of such gambling), arising out of any of the activities described in paragraph (1)(A) (i) or (ii); or

"(II) content, provided by another person, that advertises or promotes non-Internet gambling activity that is lawful under Federal law and the law of the State in which such gambling activity is conducted.

"(ii) ELIGIBILITY.—An interactive computer service is described in this clause only if the provider—

"(I) maintains and implements a written or electronic policy that requires the provider to terminate the account of a subscriber of its system or network expeditiously following the receipt by the provider of a notice described in paragraph (2)(B) alleging that such subscriber maintains a website on a computer server controlled or operated by the provider for the purpose of engaging in advertising or promotion of non-Internet gambling activity prohibited by a Federal law or a law of the State in which such activity is conducted;

"(II) with respect to the particular material or activity at issue, has not knowingly permitted its computer server to be used to engage in the advertising or promotion of non-Internet gambling activity that the provider knows is prohibited by a Federal law or a law of the State in which the activity is conducted, with the specific intent that such server be used for such purpose; and

"(III) at reasonable cost, offers residential customers of the provider's Internet access service, if the provider provides Internet access service to such customers, computer software, or another filtering or blocking system that includes the capability of filtering or blocking access by minors to online Internet gambling sites that violate this section.

"(C) NOTICE TO INTERACTIVE COMPUTER SERVICE PROVIDERS.—

"(i) NOTICE FROM FEDERAL LAW ENFORCEMENT AGENCY.—If an interactive computer service provider receives from a Federal law enforcement agency, acting within its authority and jurisdiction, a written or electronic notice described in paragraph (2)(B), that a particular online site residing on a computer server owned, controlled, or operated by or for the provider is being used by another person to advertise or promote non-Internet gambling activity that violates a Federal law prohibiting or regulating gambling or gambling-related activities, the provider shall expeditiously take the actions described in paragraph (2)(A) (i) or (ii) with respect to the advertising or promotion identified in the notice.

"(ii) NOTICE FROM STATE LAW ENFORCEMENT AGENCY.—If an interactive computer service provider receives from a State law enforcement agency, acting within its authority and jurisdiction, a written or electronic notice described in paragraph (2)(B), that a particular online site residing on a computer server owned, controlled, or operated by or for the provider is being used by another person to advertise or promote non-Internet gambling activity that is conducted in that State and that violates a law of that State prohibiting or regulating gambling or gambling-related activities, the provider shall expeditiously take the actions described in paragraph (2)(A) (i) or (ii) with respect to the advertising or promotion identified in the notice.

"(D) INJUNCTIVE RELIEF.—The United States, or a State law enforcement agency, acting within its authority and jurisdiction, may, not less than 24 hours following the issuance to an interactive computer service provider of a notice described in paragraph (2)(B), in a civil action, obtain a temporary restraining order, or an injunction, to prevent the use of the interactive computer service by another person to advertise or promote non-Internet gambling activity that violates a Federal law, or a law of the State in which such activity is conducted that prohibits or regulates gambling or gambling-related activities, as applicable. The procedures described in paragraph (3)(D) shall apply to actions brought under this subparagraph, and the relief in such actions shall be limited to—

"(i) an order requiring the provider to remove or disable access to the advertising or promotion of non-Internet gambling activity that violates Federal law, or the law of the State in which such activity is conducted, as applicable, at a particular online site residing on a computer server controlled or operated by the provider;

"(ii) an order restraining the provider from providing access to an identified subscriber of the system or network of the provider, if the court determines that such subscriber maintains a website on a computer server controlled or operated by the provider that the subscriber is knowingly using or knowingly permitting to be used to advertise or promote non-Internet gambling activity that violates Federal law or the law of the State in which such activity is conducted; and

"(iii) an order restraining the provider of the content of the advertising or promotion of such illegal gambling activity from disseminating such advertising or promotion on the computer server controlled or operated by the provider of such interactive computer service.

"(E) APPLICABILITY.—The provisions of subparagraphs (C) and (D) do not apply to the content described in subparagraph (B)(i)(II).

"(5) EFFECT ON OTHER LAW.—

"(A) IMMUNITY FROM LIABILITY FOR COMPLIANCE.—An interactive computer service provider shall not be liable for any damages, penalty, or forfeiture, civil or criminal, under Federal or State law for taking in good faith any action described in paragraph (2)(A) to comply with a notice described in paragraph (2)(B), or complying with any court order issued under paragraph (3).

"(B) DISCLAIMER OF OBLIGATIONS.—Nothing in this section may be construed to impose or authorize an obligation on an interactive computer service provider described in paragraph (1)(B)—

"(i) to monitor material or use of its service; or

"(ii) except as required by a notice or an order of a court under this subsection, to gain access to, to remove, or to disable access to material.

"(C) RIGHTS OF SUBSCRIBERS.—Nothing in this section may be construed to prejudice the right of a subscriber to secure an appropriate determination, as otherwise provided by law, in a Federal court or in a State or local tribunal or agency, that the account of such subscriber should not be terminated pursuant to this subsection, or should be restored.

"(e) AVAILABILITY OF RELIEF.—The availability of relief under subsections (c) and (d) shall not depend on, or be affected by, the initiation or resolution of any action under subsection (b), or under any other provision of Federal or State law.

"(f) APPLICABILITY.—

"(1) IN GENERAL.—Subject to paragraph (2), the prohibition in this section does not apply to—

"(A) any otherwise lawful bet or wager that is placed, received, or otherwise made wholly intrastate for a State lottery, or for a multi-State lottery operated jointly between 2 or more States in conjunction with State lotteries if—

"(i) each such lottery is expressly authorized, and licensed or regulated, under applicable State law;

"(ii) the bet or wager is placed on an interactive computer service that uses a private network or a closed-loop subscriber based service regulated and operated by the State lottery or its expressly designated agent for such activity;

"(iii) each person placing or otherwise making that bet or wager—

"(I) is physically located when such bet or wager is placed at a facility that is open to the general public; or

"(II) recieves from the State lottery a user name and password specific to the individual player for use in betting and wagering in the State lottery or multi-State lottery; and

"(iv) each such lottery complies with sections 1301 through 1304, and other applicable provisions of Federal law;

"(B) any otherwise lawful bet or wager that is placed, received, or otherwise made on an interstate or intrastate basis on a live horse or a live dog race or on jai alai, or the sending, receiving, or inviting of information assisting in the placing of such a bet or wager, if such bet or wager, or the transmission of such information, as applicable, is—

"(i) expressly authorized, and licensed or regulated by the State in which such bet or wager is received, under applicable Federal and such State's laws;

"(ii) placed on a closed-loop subscriber-based service;

"(iii) initiated from a State in which betting or wagering on that same type of live horse or live dog racing or on jai alai is lawful and received in a State in which such betting or wagering is lawful;

"(iv) subject to the regulatory oversight of the State in which the bet or wager is received and subject by such State to minimum control standards for the accounting, regulatory inspection, and auditing of all such bets or wagers transmitted from 1 State to another; and

"(v) in the case of—

"(I) live horse racing, made in accordance with the Interstate Horse Racing Act of 1978 (15 U.S.C. 3001 et seq.); or

"(II) live dog racing, subject to consent agreements that are comparable to those required by the Interstate Horse Racing Act of 1978, approved by the appropriate State regulatory agencies, in the State in which the live dog race takes place, and in the State in which the bet or wager is accepted;

"(C) any otherwise lawful bet or wager that is placed, received, or otherwise made wholly intrastate, or the sending, receiving, or inviting of information assisting in the placing of such a bet or wager, if such bet or wager, or the transmission of such information, as applicable is—

"(i) expressly authorized, and licensed or regulated by the State in which such bet or water is initiated and received, under applicable Federal and such State's laws; and

"(ii) placed on a closed-loop subscriber based service; or

"(D) any otherwise lawful bet or wager that is placed, received, or otherwise made for a fantasy sports league game or contest.

"(2) BETS OR WAGERS MADE BY AGENTS OR PROXIES.—

"(A) IN GENERAL.—Paragraph (1) does not apply in any case in which a bet or wager is placed, received, or otherwise made by the use of an agent or proxy using the Internet or an interactive computer service.

"(B) QUALIFICATION.—Nothing in this paragraph may be construed to prohibit the owner operator of a parimutuel wagering facility that is licensed by a State from employing an agent in the operation of the account wagering system owned or operated by the parimutuel facility.

"(3) ADVERTISING AND PROMOTION.—The prohibition of subsection (b)(1)(B) does not apply to advertising, promotion, or other communication by, or authorized by, anyone licensed to operate a gambling business in a State.

"(g) RULE OF CONSTRUCTION.—Nothing in this section may be construed to affect any prohibition or remedy applicable to a person engaged in a gambling business under any other provision of Federal or State law.".

(b) TECHNICAL AMENDMENT.—The analysis for chapter 50 of title 18, United States Code, is amended by adding at the end the following:

"1085. Internet gambling.".

SEC. 3. REPORT ON ENFORCEMENT.

Not later than 3 years after the date of enactment of this Act, the Attorney General shall submit to Congress a report, which shall include—

(1) an analysis of the problems, if any, associated with enforcing section 1085 of title 18, United States Code, as added by section 2 of this Act;

(2) recommendations for the best use of the resources of the Department of Justice to enforce that section; and

(3) an estimate of the amount of activity and money being used to gamble on the Internet.

SEC. 4. SEVERABILITY.

If any provision of this Act, an amendment made by this Act, or the application of such provision or amendment to any person or circumstance is held to be unconstitutional, the remainder of this Act, the amendments made by this Act, and the application of this Act and the provisions of such amendments to any other person or circumstance shall not be affected thereby.

○

Mr. CHABOT. Since our last hearing on this matter, the issues really have not changed. Illegal gambling sites abound on the Internet. Earlier this year, an FBI study reported growth from $300 million in 1998 to $651 million in 1999. Bear Stearns and Company, Inc., has just released a report that there are now 650 Internet gambling websites, and that the industry earned $1.2 billion in total revenue last year. Many predict that given its explosive rate of growth, this could soon easily become a $10 billion a year enterprise.

When Representatives Goodlatte and LoBiondo first introduced legislation 3 years ago, there were less than 30 gambling websites. Now, there are close to 700. Online casino operators have created what some have dubbed the virtual strip.

Most of these casinos are organized and operated from tropical offshore locations, where the operators are free from both State and Federal interference. Among the most popular locales are Antigua,

St. Martin, and Costa Rica. Earlier this year, Australia and New Zealand announced that they intend to become choice locations for Internet gambling operations, with plans to regulate Internet casino operators. However, the Prime Minister of Australia has since disavowed his support of legalization, citing concerns that the Internet would exacerbate gambling addiction.

There are other considerations, as well. First, security on bets placed over this unregulated segment of the Internet is ineffective, and unlike traditional regulated casinos, Internet operators have no demonstrated ability or requirement to verify a participant's age or identification. Moreover, virtual casino winners are unable to guarantee that they will ever collect their winnings. If the house loses, its operators can simply shut down their sites and begin anew. Newspaper articles across the country have already reported stories of Internet operators who simply took the money and ran. Anti-gambling activists also fear that cyber gambling will create a new generation of gambling addicts, computer-savvy youths, able to bankrupt themselves and their families from the comfort of their own homes.

As we all know, an overwhelming majority of State legislatures and referendum voters have rejected gambling beyond highly-regulated State lotteries, track betting, and Indian gaming. These States have every right to be able to enforce their laws in this area. However, States are now confronted with enforcement problems unique to the burgeoning Internet.

As a result, State Attorneys General are becoming increasingly frustrated in their attempts to prevent illegal gambling from permeating their borders. Some have tried to charge Internet gambling providers with violations of State consumer fraud laws, but jurisdictional issues and other problems have thwarted these efforts. To exacerbate this problem, Attorneys General report that citizens often are completely unaware that gambling on the Internet is illegal, even if those same people know that their home State does not allow gaming. Recently, the office of the Minnesota Attorney General felt compelled to create a web page warning Minnesotans of the illegality of online gambling.

As I have already stated, the Federal Government traditionally leaves gambling regulation to the State legislatures. In fact, the last two Federal commissions Congress created to look into gambling have concluded that States are best equipped to regulate gambling within their own borders and recommended that Congress continue to defer to the States in this respect.

In this spirit, the Federal Government has generally deferred to the authority of States to determine the type and amount of gambling permitted. For over 100 years, Congress has only acted to assist States in enforcing their respective policies on gambling when new developments in technology, such as telephones and now the Internet, have compromised the effectiveness of State gambling laws.

Today, we have been presented with a great opportunity to vet the issues associated with this bill and hear from both sides about how Congress can most effectively aid States in enforcing their laws and protect consumers from potentially devastating online fraud.

I would like to take this opportunity to thank Congressmen Goodlatte and LoBiondo for their leadership on this issue in the House and Senator Kyl, who we also expect to be here this afternoon, for his tireless dedication to Internet gambling legislation in the Senate. I know that you have worked long and hard to come up with a fair and balanced piece of legislation.

Are there any other members of the panel that would like to give an opening statement? Mr. Scott?

Mr. SCOTT. Thank you, Mr. Chairman. I appreciate your convening this hearing on the Internet Gambling Prohibition Act of 1999 in Chairman McCollum's absence. Although it is a bit unusual for the subcommittee to hold a hearing on a bill that it has already marked up, I also want to express my appreciation to Chairman McCollum and to Chairman Hyde for their recognition of the importance of holding a hearing before proceeding with full committee consideration of the bill.

I have reviewed information from prior hearings and have spoken with a number of individuals on how the bill will operate, yet this information does not adequately address the questions I have about how this bill will work. Given how lucrative the potential is for gambling over the Internet, I certainly cannot see how law enforcement can hope to prevent the barrage of gambling opportunities that will be made available by people from places where laws of the United States do not apply.

The FBI reported earlier this year that gambling over the Internet more than doubled in the last year, from $300 million in 1998 to $651 million in 1999. Others have estimated, as you have indicated, that the industry will grow into the billions in very short order. So I expect that even if we are successful in closing down sites in the United States and in cooperative countries, this will only tend to increase the profit opportunities for those who operate in uncooperative countries, especially those that the United States considers so-called rogue countries.

In addition to the technical concerns I have about the bill, I have other concerns with the bill's effectiveness in prohibiting gambling on the Internet. As a result of the exceptions in the bill for horse racing, dog racing, jai alai, and fantasy sports leagues, I have concerns about whether the bill will actually proliferate rather than prohibit gambling opportunities on the Internet. I also share the Department of Justice's concern that because of the existing Wire Communications Act, this bill will set up a dual, if not conflicting, system of enforcement, depending on how one gambles illegally on the Internet or over the phone or over some other medium.

Another question I have is why the bill makes activities for certain Internet gambling businesses illegal while not criminalizing the activities of the individuals doing the gambling with those businesses. If we took this approach in our enforcement of drug laws, we would prosecute the seller but not the buyer in a drug transaction. If we are serious about prohibiting gambling on the Internet, we should prohibit gambling on the Internet as well as running a gambling operation. The enforcement of that would be possible because the technology of the Internet would likely be in the government's favor because activities such as illegal gambling by individuals would leave a trail back to the gambler.

Finally, I question whether there should be any need for Federal action at all in this context. Even though we have the Federal Wire Communications Act, and it has been in effect since 1961, there has been very little utilization of the law by law enforcement officials as a way of attacking illegal gambling. The regulation of gambling has traditionally been left to the States and we need to hear from our witnesses why that strategy should not continue. A State can certainly prohibit gambling over the Internet by businesses in that State and can prohibit gambling by individuals within the State. Obviously, that will not be perfect in preventing the individuals from gambling, but it would be more effective than the enforcement provisions in the bill before us.

Mr. Chairman, we have assembled a knowledgeable panel with varying views on the subject of prohibiting gambling over the Internet and I look forward to their testimony, and again, thank you for convening the meeting.

Mr. CHABOT. Thank you very much.

Mr. Gekas?

Mr. GEKAS. Yes. I thank the Chair. In the opening statements of the gentleman from Ohio and those uttered by the gentleman from Virginia, and yes, by virtue of the hearings already held in this very important issue, it has become very apparent to everyone that we do not want to disturb the States' rights to control their own destinies with respect to the horse racing enterprises and other recreational activities that take the name of gambling as their common ground.

That is good news, because we cannot predict, I believe, the final language of whatever legislation we pass, but it is now safe to predict that many of the members will stand tough on making certain that the States continue to have their decades-old prerogatives in regulating gambling in their own territories preserved sacrosanct. Therefore, I am eager to hear the witnesses' testimony, and it will take a great deal to convince me to change that aspect of our efforts here today and throughout the remainder of the session. I thank the chair.

Mr. CHABOT. Thank you very much, Mr. Gekas.

Mr. Goodlatte, did you want to make a statement at this time or did you want to— —

Mr. GOODLATTE. I think I will wait.

Mr. CHABOT. Thank you very much.

Mr. CHABOT. We have four panels here this afternoon, so we are going to try to move through these at a fairly expeditious pace. On our first panel, we have one witness, who we will refer to as John Doe this afternoon. He is from San Diego, California. Last year, this young man became addicted to Internet gambling, ran up a $5,000 debt on his father's credit card playing Internet blackjack, and became so despondent as a result that he contemplated suicide. We appreciate his willingness and his courage to step forward and tell his story here this afternoon. We appreciate it very much and we will defer to you at this time.

STATEMENT OF JOHN DOE, INTERNET GAMBLING ADDICT, SAN DIEGO, CA

Mr. DOE. Well, I have been an avid gambler since I was 14 years old. Maybe the fact I was born in Las Vegas is why I have gambling in my blood. As a big fan of Las Vegas-style games, I would go to the racetrack and bet on the horses and Las Vegas to gamble before I was 18 years old. When I was 18 years old, which is the legal age to gamble in California, I would visit the Indian reservations here in San Diego and play blackjack, and the only drawback, that it cost 50 cents per hand to play, which is how the Indian tribes made their money. I would go out there about once a week sometimes, once every 2 weeks and play, and I would win money about one out of three times, which kept me coming back for more action.

I was surfing the web one day back in 1996 when I came across a banner ad for Intercasino.com that promised lots of winners and big cash payoffs in its Las Vegas style casino. Intrigued, I clicked the banner which brought me to the website. Fueled by my passion for Las Vegas games, this is when my whole Internet gambling addiction began, and I will have to admit that gambling for real money from the luxury and comfort of my own home was quite an exhilarating rush and experience.

The first time I gambled online, I won $400, so I thought to myself, I just made $400 in 2 hours and I did not even have to go anywhere to do it, so I thought that was pretty cool. In the months to follow, I would only allocate $100 a month for gambling on my personal credit card after making my payment to the only card company I had at the time. And for the next 12 months, I only won money about 30 percent of the time and quit playing for many months to follow after that.

In the early months of 1999, my father, aware of my inability to obtain a credit card due to a bad credit rating, he gave me his credit card to use, which had a $5,000 credit limit on it. He only authorized me to use the card for emergencies only. So now I am thinking to myself, here is a grand opportunity for me to make some big money for myself with this credit card.

So being the passionate gambler that I am, I was soon beckoned by my computer to gamble with a credit card. It is as if the computer was calling me to go to it and play blackjack, and it all went downhill from that point on. Essentially, I have control of my gambling behavior, but the presence of gambling on the Internet made it uncontrollable. It was just too easy to do. I could not stop. It got so bad that I would not have my friends over. I would sometimes hope that they would leave soon so I could indulge myself in this masochistic behavior and privacy of gambling.

So I would deposit $200 on my credit card, play it, lose it, $100, play it and lose it. Even when I was up about $500, my bets would increase in size to try to win back what I was down, and this was when I, of course, was using my father's credit card. So the very last thing I wanted to happen was to have my dad find out what I was doing with his credit card, so I changed the billing address to my house in San Diego instead of his.

You see, the way the casinos work is that they credit your credit card your winnings to balance out the debits. The only time they would mail someone a check in the mail would be if they deposited $100 and won money beyond that initial deposit, for they credit the credit card just the amount of the initial deposit and send a check for the remainder.

The more money I lost, the more chips I would buy on the credit card to try to win them back. I was chasing my losses, very much so. One thing led to another, and within a period of just 3 weeks, I had maxed out my father's $5,000 credit card. I was so distraught and scared that he would flip his lid when he found out what I was doing that I thought about suicide as an escape route for that. I was really depressed, nervous, and suicidal, distraught.

When my dad did find out, I just had to write him a letter explaining everything that happened to try to save myself from his wrath. I am lucky to have a great father with a big heart who does understand that gambling is a serious disease and addiction and is easily expedited with the luxury of a computer in everyone's home or business. He was mad, but very understanding and forgiving. Fortunately, he was able to get the money back that I lost since it was his card and not mine, which is lucky for me.

For people out there like myself who have a gambling problem, Internet gambling is very dangerous. It is too easy to gamble online from the comfort of your own home since all you need is a credit card, a computer, and Internet access. Like I said, the convenience of online gambling brought out an uncontrollable animal in me and I did not know when to stop. I am not obsessive-compulsive by any means, but the Internet combined with my passion for gambling, it made my behavior uncontrollable.

I am sure there are thousands of people in the world who are gambling online with money they cannot afford to lose and cannot stop. Many people have or are losing tens of thousands of dollars online and they are either severely depressed or suicidal as a result. I am here today to tell my story and hope that Congress will pass a bill making it illegal to gamble on the Internet. This could save the lives of thousands of gamblers worldwide, even teenagers, and this is a serious problem in America today and is being completely ignored. Behind the glitter and glamour of these Internet casinos lies pain, depression, regret, and even suicidal thoughts. Gambling is a serious disease, and that combined with the Internet's easy accessibility can bring financial ruin to the homes of thousands of people worldwide. It can even bring tragedy, as well.

In addition, I just want to add that many of the sites, the ones I played on were in Antigua, Canada, but they are unregulated and some of them are powered by Micro Gaming, which is a software, and there is no way to tell that it is fair for the person playing. That is unregulated. They say it has been tested by an accounting firm and what have you, but there is no way to actually prove or verify that. So, essentially, a lot of them could be fixed, and I just want to add that, too. That is all I have to say.

Mr. CHABOT. We thank you very much for your testimony.

[The prepared statement of Mr. Doe follows:]

PREPARED STATEMENT OF JOHN DOE, INTERNET GAMBLING ADDICT, SAN DIEGO, CA

I have been an avid gambler since I was fourteen years old.. Maybe the fact that I was born in Las Vegas is why I have gambling in my blood. As a big fan of Las Vegas style games, I would go to the racetrack and bet on the horses and to Las

Vegas to gamble before I was eighteen years old. When I was eighteen years old, which is the legal age to gamble in California, I would visit the Indian reservations here in San Diego and play blackjack. The only drawback was that it cost $.50 per hand to play, which is how the Indian tribes made their money. I would go out there about once a week—sometimes once every two weeks—and play. I would win money there about one out of every three times, which kept me coming back for more action.

I was surfing the web one day back in '96 when I came across an enticing banner ad for Intercasino.com that promised lots of winners and big cash payoffs in its Las Vegas style casino. Intrigued, I clicked the banner which brought me to their website. Fueled by my passion for Las Vegas games, this is when my whole Internet gambling addiction began. I'll have to admit that gambling for real money from the luxury and comfort of my own home was quite an exhilarating rush. The first time I gambled online I won $400. I thought to myself, "I just made $400 in two hours and didn't even have to leave the house to do it! How cool!" In the months to follow, I would only allocate $100 a month for gambling after making my payment to my one-and-only credit card company at the time. For the next 12 months I only won money about 30% of the time and quit playing for many months to follow.

In the early months of 1999 my father, aware of my inability to obtain a credit card due to a public tax lien, gave me his credit card to use which had a $5000 credit line on it. He only authorized me to use the card for emergencies only. Now I'm thinking to myself, "Here's a grand opportunity for me to make some big bucks for myself!" Being the passionate gambler that I am, was soon beckoned by my computer to gamble with the credit card. It's as if the computer was calling me to go to it and play blackjack . . . It all went downhill from this point on. I have control of my gambling behavior, but the presence of gambling on the Internet made it uncontrollable. It was just too easy to do, and I couldn't stop. It got so bad that when I had my friends over, I would sometimes hope that they would leave soon so I could indulge myself in this masochistic behavior in privacy once again.

I would deposit $200 on my credit card, play it and lose it. $100, play it and lose it. Even when I was up about $500 my bets would increase in size to try to win back what I was down. The very last thing I wanted to happen was to have my dad find out what I was doing with his credit card, so I changed the billing address to my house in San Diego instead of his. You see, the way these casinos work is they credit your credit card your winnings to balance out the debits. The only time they would mail someone a check would be if they deposited $100 and won money beyond their initial deposit, for they credit the card just the amount of the initial deposit and send a check for the rest. The more money I lost the more chips I would buy on the credit card to try to win it back. I was chasing my losses . . . big time! Well, one thing led to another and within a period of just three weeks I had maxed out my father's $5000 credit card. I was so distraught and scared that he would flip his lid when he found out that I thought about suicide as an escape route. I was severely depressed, nervous, and suicidal.

When my dad found out, I just had to write him a letter explaining everything that happened to try to save myself from his wrath. I'm lucky to have such a great father with a big heart who understands that gambling is a serious disease and addiction. He was mad, but very understanding and forgiving. He was also able to get the money back that I lost since it was his card and not mine. Lucky for me.

For people out there like myself who have a gambling problem, Internet gambling is dangerous. It's too easy to gamble online from the comfort of your own home since all you need is a credit card, a computer, and Internet access. Like I said, the convenience of online gambling brought out an uncontrollable animal in me. I didn't know when to stop. I am not obsessive compulsive by any means, but the Internet combined with my passion for gambling made my behavior uncontrollable. I'm sure there are thousands of people in the world who are gambling online with money they can't afford to lose and cannot stop. Many people have or are losing tens of thousands of dollars online and are either severely depressed or suicidal as a result. I am here today to tell my story in hope that Congress will pass a bill making it illegal to gamble on the Internet. Not too long ago, President Bill Clinton was trying to pass a law making it illegal to gamble money over telephone lines. This bill was vetoed with the introduction of DSL and other high speed Internet access companies during this "dot.com" explosion. This could save the lives of thousands of gamblers worldwide—even teenagers. This is a serious problem in America today and is being completely ignored. Behind the glitter and glamour of these Internet casinos lies pain, depression, regret, even suicidal thoughts. Gambling is a serious disease that, combined with the Internet's easy accessability, can bring financial ruin to the homes of thousands of people worldwide—even tragedy.

Mr. CHABOT. The panel members may have questions for you, and I will start out here. We have 5 minutes to ask you questions.

First of all, were you aware, or what was your understanding of the legality of what you were involved in, and would it have made a difference if some of what you were doing was illegal? Would that have made a difference to you, do you think, at the time or subsequently?

Mr. DOE. If it was illegal? Sure, it would. If a bill is passed making it illegal, then I would not be prone to do it.

Mr. CHABOT. Did you have other associates or other friends, or do you know other people that were in similar situations as yours? Were there other people that——

Mr. DOE. No.

Mr. CHABOT. How did you first become aware that this was available to you out there? How did you first become aware that this was something that you could become involved in on the Internet?

Mr. DOE. I came across a banner for a casino one day when I was surfing the Internet. I am online pretty much every day.

Mr. CHABOT. Did you get any kind of counseling, or are you in something that helps you to deal with that?

Mr. DOE. No.

Mr. CHABOT. I do not have any other questions, so I am going to defer to Mr. Scott at this point.

Mr. SCOTT. Thank you. Mr. Doe, you said if it had been illegal to gamble over the Internet, you would not have done it. Are you aware that there is nothing in the bill before us that would prohibit you from gambling on the Internet? It would not be illegal for you to gamble. It would be illegal for the companies to run the operations. So if you could find a casino on the web, there would be no prohibition against you gambling. Are you aware that that is part of the bill?

Mr. DOE. Right.

Mr. SCOTT. Then it would not prohibit you from gambling on the Internet.

Mr. DOE. What would not prohibit me?

Mr. SCOTT. You said if it had been illegal for you, you would not have done it. This bill does not provide any prohibition against you gambling on the Internet. It prohibits a business from setting up a website on which you could gamble, but to the extent that we cannot shut them down, there is no prohibition in the bill against you gambling. Do you think there ought to be a provision in the bill to prohibit the gambler from gambling on the Internet?

Mr. DOE. State regulated, yes, sure. That would help out significantly, I think.

Mr. SCOTT. What do you have to say about the exceptions in the bill for horse racing, where you could do horse racing, jai alai, and dog race——

Mr. DOE. Sports betting.

Mr. SCOTT [continuing]. Fantasy sports betting, that the bill has carve-outs so that you could do those. You just could not do anything else. Do you think those carve-outs ought to be eliminated so that you could not do horse race betting from your home?

Mr. DOE. I think that can develop into a severe problem, so that should be banned, too. I personally did not bet on sports online or horse racing or anything like that, but I know it is out there. So I would be in favor of that, too.

Mr. SCOTT. No further questions, Mr. Chairman. Thank you. Thank you for your testimony.

Mr. CHABOT. Thank you.

Mr. Gekas?

Mr. GEKAS. Yes, Mr. Chairman. If the whole thing were declared illegal and horse racing were declared illegal and all forms of gambling, you could still go to Las Vegas, could you not?

Mr. DOE. Sure.

Mr. GEKAS. Do you believe that if everything else were unavailable to you, you would never be tempted to go to Las Vegas to engage in whatever enterprises there were there? Do you think that you still would be able to resist the temptation to go to Las Vegas?

Mr. DOE. I would try to go out there once every couple months or so for a vacation, and I do gamble when I am out there in Las Vegas, sure, but——

Mr. GEKAS. If you came to it, you would be able to use a credit card for that purpose.

Mr. DOE. I use my ATM card, but I would not use a credit card.

Mr. GEKAS. What I am getting at is that you personally were unable to resist the temptation to use the credit card and your resources on the Internet, is that not correct?

Mr. DOE. That is correct.

Mr. GEKAS. But you still succumbed to the temptation to gamble by going to the Indian casinos, you said, by going to Las Vegas.

Mr. DOE. Yes.

Mr. GEKAS. So it becomes a matter of personal discipline and personal devotion to yourself to try to do less gambling or no gambling at all, is that not correct?

Mr. DOE. That is true, but the main issue is the Internet is so convenient. It is right there in your own home.

Mr. GEKAS. In other words, you are tempted by what is available, is that what you are saying?

Mr. DOE. Yes.

Mr. GEKAS. And you want society to be less tempting to you, is that what you are really saying?

Mr. DOE. I want the States to have some control of that and——

Mr. GEKAS. States do have control of their enterprises, and that is what part of the whole situation is in the legislation that we are attempting. I am simply trying to elicit from you whether you can agree with me that a large portion of your problem and other persons who become addicted to it is not the fact that the temptation is there, because there will always be some temptations, will there not?

Mr. DOE. Right.

Mr. GEKAS. But rather, the inability to resist the temptation, which becomes a matter of personal character and ability to withstand temptation that can be destructive, do you not agree?

Mr. DOE. I agree, but I came here today to—I had control of my gambling until I discovered Internet gambling. Other than that, I was in control of it.

Mr. GEKAS. You felt you had control of it until——

Mr. DOE. And then I went to Internet casinos.

Mr. GEKAS [continuing]. Until the Internet, is that it?

Mr. DOE. Right, until I discovered the online gambling. It was so convenient and it was just right there. When you are down, you are going to chase what you are down and try to win it back.

Mr. GEKAS. Do you want to tell us when is the last time you placed a bet of any type? You do not have to tell us. Have you placed a bet in the last month?

Mr. DOE. Yes, I have.

Mr. GEKAS. Do you want to tell us where and how, I mean, what type?

Mr. DOE. It was——

Mr. SCOTT. Do you want to read him his rights first? [Laughter.]

Mr. GEKAS. You do not have to answer any of these, and I do not want to be accused of abusing a witness, either. But you say you have in the last month placed a bet?

Mr. DOE. Yes, I have.

Mr. GEKAS. Do you want to tell us how much?

Mr. DOE. It was—I allocated $100 and lost that and said, forget about it.

Mr. GEKAS. And you did not do this on the Internet?

Mr. DOE. It was on the Internet.

Mr. GEKAS. It was on the Internet?

Mr. DOE. It was on a different website, yes.

Mr. GEKAS. So, in effect, you are telling us that your appetite or your addiction is not fully controllable by yourself. That is, you are still tempted.

Mr. DOE. I think the ease of access would promote gambling more on line. It is convenient. All you need is a credit card. There are many kids out there that probably are not even old enough to gamble that steal their parents' credit card when they are asleep or what have you, go online and gamble and win money, or most of—in 99 percent of the cases, lose money.

Mr. GEKAS. That is a good point. That is a worrisome feature of all of your testimony.

Mr. DOE. And that is the main issue that needs to be addressed. It is so easy to do, and without the ease of use.

Mr. GEKAS. I have no further questions.

Mr. CHABOT. Thank you, Mr. Gekas.

Mr. Weiner?

Mr. WEINER. Thank you, Mr. Chabot.

John, thank you for taking the time. This has been helpful. You said that the website where you gambled was based in Antigua?

Mr. DOE. Yes.

Mr. WEINER. Did you care where it was based?

Mr. DOE. No.

Mr. WEINER. If there was a website that was based in Paris or in Spain or in South America, you would have had the same problem with those sites so long as they offered you the services that you wanted to gamble on?

Mr. DOE. Yes, I would.

Mr. WEINER. So these temptations that were coming at you were well beyond our shores, but they were just as powerful on you whether they were in Pennsylvania or whether they were in the

Philippines? I mean, essentially, where these things—and in the case of the Internet, are you fairly proficient with the Internet?

Mr. DOE. Yes, quite savvy.

Mr. WEINER. In the case with the Internet, you can literally get products and services and writings and photographs from all around the world with the Internet.

Mr. DOE. Yes.

Mr. WEINER. And that is one of the things that has led to the explosion of the Internet, is this free transfer of commerce, the free transfer of ideas and the like. The reason I asked you this is one of the things we are wrestling with here is how to act on an Internet policy in general, and in general, we have said in this committee and said in this Congress and, frankly, the administration at the White House has said similarly, we are going to take a step back. There are going to be some bad things that are going to happen. People are going to have access to pornographic images that we are not going to like. People are going to post weapons to make bombs that we are not going to like. People are going to be exposed to gambling that might not be appropriate for them to be exposed to. But generally, we have taken the position that, hey, this is something that in its totality is worth preserving, A, and B, we in government really do not know what the heck to do to try to deal with this global transfer of information.

So with that being said, I guess the question I would ask you, as a consumer of the Internet, are there other things on the Internet that you think we should also crack down on because they provide perhaps some deleterious effect to our communities? Should we not have, perhaps, should we prohibit the transfer of pornographic images or the like?

Mr. DOE. Sure.

Mr. WEINER. Is this something you have given some thought to since you have been impacted so adversely by this little corner of the Internet, and since you use the Internet in its totality, I thought you might have given some thought to that.

Mr. DOE. Yes. Well, the Internet gives a consumer more choices vis-a-vis as to buy online. I think that is great. There are people out there who are pornographic website addicts per se, but it does not ruin them financially. So I think the only issue is taking control of—doing something about the Internet gaming.

Mr. WEINER. Got you.

Mr. DOE. I know President Clinton tried to pass a bill making it illegal to gamble over a telephone line a couple years back, but with the introduction of DSL and other online access, that bill became infeasible.

Mr. WEINER. Well, it is already illegal to call your bookie and place a bet, but John, let me ask you another question that perhaps is related. Is there a certain type of gambling that you would like to do, and I apologize if you covered this before I got here. Was there a blackjack or slots? What was the game that was your choice, or did you play many different ones?

Mr. DOE. Blackjack and roulette.

Mr. WEINER. Now, if there were other types of gambling that were available, for example, we particularly take note in this legislation of horse racing and dog racing, and I guess jai alai is also included, if there were other types of gambling available, would you simply move? Do you have a desire to gamble or is it just a desire to play blackjack?

Mr. DOE. It is mainly a desire to gamble. My game of choice—well, it is my desire to gamble and win money, so it is my passion for gambling that was driven uncontrollably with the ease of the Internet.

Mr. WEINER. So if you had a sure shot on a 25-to-1 horse that you thought for sure was going to win, you would have a desire to gamble on that horse race, just like you would have a desire to double-down on 11?

Mr. DOE. I would consider that.

Mr. WEINER. Thank you, Mr. Chairman.

Mr. CHABOT. Thank you, Mr. Weiner.

Mr. Coble?

Mr. COBLE. Thank you, Mr. Chairman.

Mr. Doe, Merle Haggard, the country balladeer, do you know him by name? Is the name known to you?

Mr. DOE. No, sir.

Mr. COBLE. Merle Haggard recorded a song once entitled "The Kentucky Gambler," and the concluding lyrics of the song were, "But a gambler loses much more than he wins," and I assume that you would concur with that, based upon your unfortunate experience.

Mr. DOE. Yes, sir.

Mr. COBLE. I came in late, too, Mr. Doe. Is it your belief that you remain addicted, or do you think you have overcome the addiction? You may have covered that earlier. If so, I apologize.

Mr. DOE. I think my drive for gambling and my passion for that, combined with my—I like to surf the web. So just surfing the web combined with my passion for gambling creates disaster. Even for those that try to quit gambling, the computer will beckon them as it did myself.

Mr. COBLE. The tempting snares are still there, I take it.

Mr. DOE. Right.

Mr. COBLE. No, I believe in response to the chairman's question, you said that you have not sought counseling for this addiction?

Mr. DOE. No.

Mr. COBLE. Have you considered seeking counseling, and I do not mean to prescribe what you should do, but it appears to me that if this continues to be a problem with you, then counseling might well assuage the discomfort. It might cure you.

Mr. DOE. I would consider that.

Mr. COBLE. I think everything else regarding the bill, Mr. Chairman, has been pretty well laid down. One final question, Mr. Doe. I assume your daddy no longer surrenders his card to you, or does he? [Laughter.]

I did not mean that to be humorous, but does he surrender his card to you from time to time now?

Mr. DOE. No.

Mr. COBLE. That is probably a good idea, at least at this juncture. Thank you, Mr. Doe, for being with us. Thank you, Mr. Chairman.

Mr. CHABOT. Thank you, Mr. Coble, and we thank you, Mr. Doe.

Mr. GOODLATTE. Mr. Chairman?

Mr. SCOTT. Mr. Chairman, I would ask unanimous consent that Mr. Goodlatte be able to participate as a member of the subcommittee.

Mr. CHABOT. Without objection. The chair recognizes Mr. Goodlatte for 5 minutes.

Mr. GOODLATTE. Mr. Chairman, thank you, and I thank the ranking member, as well, for the courtesy extended.

Mr. Doe, I want to thank you for coming and testifying today. I know this is a personally troubling and embarrassing experience that you have been through and it has caused you a great deal of difficulty, so to come here and share your thoughts with us is valuable.

Let me ask you, you are, as I understand it, from the State of California?

Mr. DOE. Yes.

Mr. GOODLATTE. California does not have legalized casino gambling, does it?

Mr. DOE. It does, but it is on an Indian reservation.

Mr. GOODLATTE. Only on Indian reservations, not in other parts of the State where you live, is that correct?

Mr. DOE. That is correct.

Mr. GOODLATTE. So the problem that you encountered was that here was something that you have this really strong attraction to, an addiction, if you will, that was right there in your home. Where do you keep your computer, in your living room or your family room or your bedroom?

Mr. DOE. The living room.

Mr. GOODLATTE. So right there in your living room, you could do things that otherwise you would have to travel a distance to do, and you could go right there online and there was no one. You did not have to interface with anybody. You did not have to talk to a croupier or a blackjack dealer or anybody. You could just bring it right up online and——

Mr. DOE. I did not have to drive anywhere.

Mr. GOODLATTE. With your father's credit card, you were in business and could run up a substantial debt right there at home, is that right?

Mr. DOE. Yes,

Mr. GOODLATTE. Even though the State of California prohibits those kind of operations from being offered in your community and other communities around the State. Was that the main problem with this from your standpoint, the ease with which you could do that?

Mr. DOE. That was the main problem.

Mr. GOODLATTE. Now, when you were dealing with these folks, did you know anything about who they were, whether they were regulated by anybody or whether the odds that you were getting when you gambled were fair or whether or not, in fact, if you won a substantial amount of money that you would get paid?

Mr. DOE. I did have an understanding of how the system worked. They credited your credit card up to your initial deposit, which is——

Mr. GOODLATTE. Right, but you were not in a building with them where you knew people were regulating them, and if you won, you would be assured of getting your winnings, and if you were losing, you were assured that the odds were fair odds regulated by the State——

Mr. DOE. Yes.

Mr. GOODLATTE [continuing]. Because, in fact, they were not, were they?

Mr. DOE. No, I do not believe so.

Mr. GOODLATTE. They are not regulated by anybody, and they are located in many instances offshore in different places. Now, in order to do this, you had to be able to send them money, is that right?

Mr. DOE. Right.

Mr. GOODLATTE. Unlike a casino that you might walk into in Las Vegas where you could carry cash in or bring a check and get that cash or whatever, you had to have some way to send them money, and that is where the credit card came in. If you did not have that credit card, you would not be able to gamble on the Internet, is that correct?

Mr. DOE. Correct, yes. They also offered a Western Union wire transfer.

Mr. GOODLATTE. So you could wire them money——

Mr. DOE. True.

Mr. GOODLATTE [continuing]. But those were the only ways that you could deal with them, is that right?

Mr. DOE. Yes.

Mr. GOODLATTE. We thank you. The State of California does not allow jai alai gambling, does it? Do you know what jai alai is?

Mr. DOE. No, I do not, sir.

Mr. GOODLATTE. It is a sport sort of like racquetball with big baskets. I am going to offend somebody here who is a jai alai fan. [Laughter.]

It is common in Florida and some other States where it is legal and you are allowed to gamble there, but that is not allowed in California to your knowledge, is it?

Mr. DOE. Not to my knowledge.

Mr. GOODLATTE. Under this bill, that is not an exception. You could not gamble on jai alai in California. The bill only allows that to take place in the States where it is legal under what is called a closed-loop system, and it could also be allowed in another State that might have what is called an off-track betting site for horse racing or the State in which the betting was legal, but not in other States. It is not a blanket nationwide exemption.

You may not well know that aspect of the bill, but I just want to point out, for the benefit of the gentleman from New York, that these exceptions are designed to take into account gambling that is legal within certain States and to permit that to continue to be legal even when conducted on the Internet, provided it is for the benefit of those States' residents and other States that have entered into agreements with those States to permit it in their States, like an off-track betting site operates.

Mr. Chairman, I thank you, and I thank you, Mr. Doe, for your participation.

Mr. CHABOT. Thank you, Mr. Goodlatte. I think that is the last question for this particular witness. At this time, I have some special instructions that I ask the media's cooperation, and that is that as the witness exits the room, we would request that the TV cameras be directed up here to the chair, or if you would prefer not to direct them at me, you can direct them at Mr. Scott here, but that you not direct them at the witness. And as far as the cameras, the still photography, if you would not take pictures of the witness as he exits the room here. So if you could direct the cameras, that is fine, and no still photography, please.

[Pause.]

Mr. CHABOT. I want to thank the media's cooperation. As soon as the screens are removed, we will introduce the second panel.

Mr. WEINER. Mr. Goodlatte, would you like to go behind the screen? [Laughter.]

Mr. CHABOT. We would like him to be behind a screen, but he would not go along with it. [Laughter.]

The second panel, and only half of it is here right now, we expect Senator Kyl to be along at some point this afternoon. He is held up by votes over in the Senate. He is the principal sponsor of the Internet Gambling Prohibition Act of 1999 over in the Senate.

So the other half of the panel is a member of the Judiciary Committee, the Honorable Bob Goodlatte. He is United States Representative from the Sixth Congressional District in the Commonwealth of Virginia. On the Judiciary Committee, Representative Goodlatte serves on the Constitution Subcommittee, the Courts and Intellectual Property Subcommittee, and the Immigration Subcommittee. On the Agriculture Committee, he is the chairman of the Department Operations, Oversight, Nutrition, and Forestry Subcommittee and also serves on the Livestock and Horticulture Subcommittee. Mr. Goodlatte has been a leader in Congress on a number of Internet and high-tech issues. Bob?

STATEMENT OF HON. ROBERT W. GOODLATTE, A REPRESENTATIVE IN CONGRESS FROM THE STATE OF VIRGINIA

Mr. GOODLATTE. Mr. Chairman, thank you for holding this hearing. I want to thank your and Chairman McCollum's willingness to have this forum for discussion and a dialogue on a topic that is of profound importance to the American people and to American ideals, the growing need for legislation to address the problem of illegal Internet gambling. I would also like to thank Senator Kyl for his leadership in the Senate on this issue. I look forward to continuing to work with him on this important matter.

The Internet is a revolutionary tool that dramatically affects the way we communicate, conduct business, and access information. As it knows no boundaries, the Internet is accessed by folks in rural and urban areas alike, in large countries as well as small. The Internet is currently expanding by leaps and bounds. However, it has not yet come close to reaching its true potential as a medium for commerce, communication, and education.

One of the main reasons that the Internet has not reached this potential is that many folks view it as a wild frontier, with no safeguards to protect children and very few legal protections to prevent online criminal activity. The ability of the World Wide Web to penetrate every home and community across the globe has both positive and negative implications. While it can be an invaluable source of information and means of communication, it can also override community values and standards, subjecting communities to whatever may or may not be found online. In short, the Internet is a challenge to the sovereignty of civilized communities, States, and nations to decide what is appropriate and decent behavior.

Gambling is an excellent example of this situation. It is currently illegal in the United States unless regulated by the States. With the development of the Internet, however, prohibitions and regulations governing gambling have been turned on their head. No longer do people have to leave the comfort of their homes and make the affirmative decision to travel to a casino. They can access the casino from their living rooms. The negative consequences of online gambling can be as detrimental to the families and communities of addictive gamblers as if a bricks and mortar casino was built right next door. Online gambling can result in addiction, bankruptcy, divorce, other family problems, despair, moral decline, crime, just as the traditional forms of gambling, the cost of which must ultimately be borne by society, and by the community in which it takes place.

I have long been a champion of the Internet and an advocate of limited government regulation of this new medium. However, that does not mean that the Internet should be a regulatory-free zone or that our existing laws should not apply to the Internet. I think we can all agree that it would be very bad public policy to allow offline activity deemed criminal by States to be freely committed online and to go unpunished simply because we are reluctant to apply our laws to the Internet.

Current law already prohibits gambling over telephone wires. However, because the Internet does not always travel over telephone wires, these laws, which were written before the invention of the World Wide Web, have become outdated. My legislation simply clarifies the state of the law by bringing the current prohibition against wireline interstate gambling up to speed with the development of new technology.

The 104th Congress created the National Gambling Impact Study Commission and charged it with conducting a comprehensive legal and factual study of gambling, including an assessment of the interstate and international effects of gambling by electronic means, including the use of interactive technologies and the Internet. According to the commission, total prohibition of gambling on the Internet, a proposition unanimously endorsed by every member of the commission, would provide law enforcement with the additional authority it needs to prosecute dishonest operators.

Contrary to federalism arguments that have been raised by the opponents of the bill, the legislation I have introduced will return control to the States by protecting the rights of citizens in each State to decide through their State legislatures if they want to allow gambling within their borders and not have that right taken away by offshore fly-by-night operators.

The bill also maintains a hands-off policy toward Internet service providers by granting them protection from liability and ensuring that they do not have to police their networks for illegal activity.

It would protect those ISPs whose facilities are used by another person to engage in Internet gambling, provided that the material is transmitted by a person other than the provider and through an automatic process.

In addition, the liability protection is contingent on the provider responding expeditiously to a notice from law enforcement that illegal gambling is occurring on their network by removing or disabling access to the site containing the illegal activity. This language is similar to the liability provisions for copyright violations included in the Digital Millennium Copyright Act enacted in 1998.

Mr. Chairman, online gambling is currently a $600 million per year business and could easily grow to $1 billion in the next few years. It is time to shine a bright light on Internet gambling in this country and put a stop to this situation before it gets any worse. The Internet Gambling Prohibition Act, which will keep children from borrowing the family credit card, as we saw here just a few minutes ago, logging onto the family computer and losing thousands of dollars all before their parents get home from work, will do that.

I want to again thank you for holding this hearing and allowing me to testify before the committee. Let me also say to the gentleman from Virginia that the original legislation submitted in the last Congress included prohibitions against the user of the Internet service and I would be happy to work with the gentleman to look at those kinds of prohibitions in the legislation if he is intent upon offering an amendment to do so.

Thank you, Mr. Chairman.

Mr. CHABOT. Thank you very much, Mr. Goodlatte.

[The prepared statement of Mr. Goodlatte follows:]

PREPARED STATEMENT OF HON. ROBERT W. GOODLATTE, A REPRESENTATIVE IN CONGRESS FROM THE STATE OF VIRGINIA

Thank you, Mr. Chairman, for agreeing to hold this hearing. I very much appreciate your willingness to have this forum for a discussion and a dialogue on a topic that is of profound importance to the American people and to American ideals: the growing need for legislation to address the problem of illegal Internet gambling. I would also like to thank Senator Kyl for his leadership in the Senate on this issue. I look forward to continuing to work with him on this very important matter.

The Internet is a revolutionary tool that dramatically affects the way we communicate, conduct business, and access information. As it knows no boundaries, the Internet is accessed by folks in rural and urban areas alike, in large countries as well as small. The Internet is currently expanding by leaps and bounds; however, it has not yet come close to reaching its true potential as a medium for commerce and communication.

One of the main reasons that the Internet has not reached this potential is that many folks view it as a wild frontier, with no safeguards to protect children and very few legal protections to prevent online criminal activity. The ability of the World Wide Web to penetrate every home and community across the globe has both positive and negative implications—while it can be an invaluable source of information and means of communication, it can also override community values and standards, subjecting them to whatever may or may not be found online. In short, the Internet is a challenge to the sovereignty of civilized communities, States, and nations to decide what is appropriate and decent behavior.

Gambling is an excellent example of this situation. It is currently illegal in the United States unless regulated by the States. With the development of the Internet, however, prohibitions and regulations governing gambling have been turned on their head. No longer do people have to leave the comfort of their homes and make the affirmative decision to travel to a casino—they can access the casino from their living rooms.

The negative consequences of online gambling can be as detrimental to the families and communities of addictive gamblers as if a bricks and mortar casino was built right next door. Online gambling can result in bankruptcy, despair, and moral decline just as with traditional forms of gambling, the costs of which must ultimately be borne by society.

I have long been a champion of the Internet and an advocate of limited government regulation of this new medium. However, that does not mean that the Internet should be a regulatory free zone or that our existing laws should not apply to the Internet. I think we can all agree that it would be very bad public policy to allow offline activity deemed criminal by states to be freely committed online and to go unpunished simply because we are reluctant to apply our laws to the Internet.

Current law *already* prohibits gambling over telephone wires. However, because the Internet does not always travel over telephone wires, these laws, which were written before the invention of the World Wide Web, have become outdated. My legislation simply clarifies the state of the law by bringing the current prohibition against wireline interstate gambling up to speed with the development of new technology.

The 104th Congress created the National Gambling Impact Study Commission and charged it with conducting a comprehensive legal and factual study of gambling, including an assessment of the interstate and international effects of gambling by electronic means, including the use of interactive technologies and the Internet. According to the Commission, "total prohibition of gambling on the Internet, a proposition unanimously endorsed by every member of the [Commission], would provide law enforcement with the additional authority it needs to prosecute dishonest operators."

Contrary to federalism arguments that have been raised by the opponents of the bill, the legislation I have introduced will return control to the states by protecting the right of citizens in each State to decide through their State legislatures if they want to allow gambling within their borders and not have that right taken away by offshore, fly-by-night operators.

The bill also maintains a hands-off policy toward Internet Service Providers by granting them protection from liability and ensuring that they do not have to police their networks for illegal activity. It would protect those ISPs whose facilities are used by another person to engage in Internet gambling, provided that the material is transmitted by a person other than the provider and through an automatic process. In addition, the liability protection is contingent on the provider responding expeditiously to a notice from law enforcement that illegal gambling is occurring on their network by removing or disabling access to the site containing the illegal activity. This language is similar to the liability provisions for copyright violations included in the Digital Millennium Copyright Act enacted in 1998.

Mr. Chairman, online gambling is currently a $200 million per year business, and could easily grow to $1 billion business in the next few years. It is time to shine a bright light on Internet gambling in this country, and to put a stop to this situation before it gets any worse. The Internet Gambling Prohibition Act, which will keep children from borrowing the family credit card, logging on to the family computer, and losing thousands of dollars all before their parents get home from work, will do just that. I want to again thank you for holding this hearing and for allowing me to testify before the Subcommittee.

Mr. CHABOT. It has been normally the policy of the committee that we do not question the members. Did you want to——

Mr. SCOTT. I just had one question. You cited the Gambling Commission. Did they look to the gambler or the business?

Mr. GOODLATTE. I do not know the exact answer to that, but I know they definitely want to have the entities banned from conducting business in the United States.

Mr. SCOTT. Thank you, Mr. Chairman.

Mr. CHABOT. At this time, we have two votes on the floor, so we are going to recess until after the second vote. As soon as the second vote is over, we will come back and continue with the hearing again.

[Recess.]

Mr. CHABOT. We are back in session. We are going to have as our first witness the Honorable Jon Kyl, United States Senator from the State of Arizona. Elected to the Senate in 1994 after four terms in the U.S. House of Representatives, Senator Kyl serves on the Judiciary, Appropriations, and Intelligence Committees. In addition, he is the chairman of the Subcommittee on Technology, Terrorism, and Government Information of the Judiciary Committee and serves as a deputy Senate whip.

Senator Kyl is the author of S. 692, the Internet Gambling Prohibition Act of 1999, which was passed by unanimous consent in the Senate in November 1999, and we welcome you here this afternoon, Senator Kyl.

Also on this panel, we have Mr. Kevin DiGregory. Mr. DiGregory is the Deputy Assistant Attorney General in the Criminal Division of the U.S. Department of Justice. He has spent his entire legal career as a trial prosecutor, beginning in 1979 in the District Attorney's Office in his native Pittsburgh, Pennsylvania. Just prior to coming to the Justice Department, he served as Janet Reno's Chief Assistant for Major Crimes in Miami, Florida.

Mr. DiGregory's current responsibilities include serving as the Department representative on the Executive Working Group for Federal, State, and Local Prosecutors. He also supervises two of the Criminal Division's litigating sections, the Computer Crime and Intellectual Property Section, and the Child Exploitation and Obscenity Section.

In the interest of time here this afternoon, we are going to have a combined panel, and our third witness will be the Honorable Jim Doyle, Attorney General of Wisconsin. General Doyle was elected Attorney General in 1990 and then reelected in 1994 and again in 1998, when he received more votes than any candidate for State office in Wisconsin history. Prior to his election as Attorney General, he served three terms as Dane County District Attorney and worked in private law practice.

General Doyle chairs the National Association of Attorneys General Internet Working Group. As a result of his leadership, Wisconsin has been on the forefront of defending itself from illegal Internet gambling operators, having filed three lawsuits to protect its citizens and enforce Wisconsin anti-gambling laws.

We will begin with Senator Kyl.

STATEMENT OF HON. JON KYL, A UNITED STATES SENATOR FROM THE STATE OF ARIZONA

Mr. KYL. Thank you very much, Mr. Chairman and Representative Scott. I am pleased to testify in support of this legislation. Let me give you a brief overview from my perspective of what happened in the Senate as a background for what the House of Representatives may wish to do, and then I would like to answer questions if there are any.

I introduced this bill in December 1995, so it has been around quite a while. We have had a couple of hearings. It has been approved twice by the Senate Judiciary Committee, and I want to emphasize that it passed the Senate unanimously. Now, we all know that sometimes things are done by unanimous consent, but it is a little different in the Senate. You have to go around and get every single Senator to sign off if you are going to do something by unanimous consent, which is what we did. We did that by working with every single group that had some interest in this legislation, and at the end of the day ensuring that, one way or another, we had a consensus develop.

Let me just give you a little perspective. When we first had testimony from the State Attorneys General, headed by Jim Doyle at that time, Attorney General Doyle came back and said that Internet gambling is really proliferating. He said that there were something like 23 of these sites on the Internet, and now I believe there are something like 700. The Department of Justice has made the point that these sites are exploding, that the impact on youth could be significant.

One of the statements from the Department of Justice says that Internet gambling has increased at an alarming rate, that the potential for operators of Internet gambling sites to successfully defraud their customers is significantly greater than with traditional casino-style gambling, that Internet gambling presents a greater danger for compulsive gamblers, and I would note a particular potential harm to minors. So that is the Justice Department, and we agree on much of the background and the necessity for this legislation.

Let me make clear that in trying to meet with different interests that were concerned about this legislation, we did not create exceptions. If we had created any exceptions, there would be no reason for the bill, because if it is possible to go into your living room and log on in your own home and do Internet gambling in any State in the union, you have just broken the entire back of this legislation. This legislation only works if all of the States operate in essentially the same way with respect to one key point, and that is no Internet gambling. So there are no exceptions to that.

This is because the Attorneys General first came to our committee and said, look, we never asked the Federal Government to take jurisdiction from us, but we are asking for help in this case because we cannot enforce the public policy of our various States against Internet gambling so long as there is anybody out there doing it, because cyberspace knows no State boundaries. So we need to bring the 1961 Telephone and Wire Act up to date—that is the sports gambling prohibition—and extend it to the casinos, these virtual casinos that are coming in from offshore. That will enable the State to enforce their State public policy against Internet gambling.

So what are these things called exceptions? What we have said is that activities like State lotteries, like parimutuel wagering, like fantasy sports, like Indian gambling, activities which are, and this is the critical phrase, otherwise lawful, activities which are otherwise lawful, will continue to be permitted. In other words, we are locking in the status quo. But the status quo does not permit Internet gambling for any of those activities. So we are not allowing any of those entities to do more than they are doing today, and we are not allowing any of them to engage in Internet gambling.

We have drawn a very firm line and said, you can continue to do what you are doing, but you cannot do Internet gambling. So they are not exceptions to this. If there were any exception, I would argue against the bill. I would vote against the bill. I would see that it never came up. There cannot be any exceptions or it will not work. But what there are is a recognition that there is otherwise lawful activity which can continue.

Just a couple of comments on our friends from the Department of Justice, because I will have to leave before I will be able to hear their testimony. But I did want to make that first point, because there is a suggestion by representatives of the Department of Justice that we expand gambling opportunities. Believe me, that is not my intention and I would not support that situation. We only permit that which is otherwise lawful.

Secondly, we do not permit conduct which has previously been deemed unacceptable in the physical world over telephone wires. Again, we only permit that which is otherwise lawful.

And finally, there is a bit of a dichotomy with the Department of Justice. It wants the bill to be technology neutral, but in a letter last year, the Department also stated it is critical that the legislation recognize that the Internet is different from prior modes of communication, that this legislation should be carefully drafted so as to avoid unduly burdening the communication medium, and we agree with that.

That is why we have established a specific enforcement mechanism that is very clear and only applies to this kind of technology. It essentially says, when the judicial authority determines that there is a violation, that is to say that one of these offshore sites is conducting a virtual casino kind of operation over the Internet, then at the point of entry into the United States, whether it is with the service provider or the switching operation, whatever it is, that service is terminated. That is the enforcement mechanism in the legislation.

Mr. Chairman, there is so much more I can say about this, but I wanted to make the point, first of all, that the Senate is now totally united behind this legislation, that we have not created any exceptions, that there cannot be any exceptions or it does not work, that we have been very mindful of the unique technology involved here, Representative Goodlatte is one of the leaders in that regard, and that our enforcement goes directly to this unique method of transmitting signals.

Finally, I think if we do not get this legislation passed this year, we are never going to get it, because the amount of money behind this is staggering. The sites have burgeoned, as I said, from 23 to 700 in just 4 years. The amount of money gambled is projected to be in the hundreds of billions of dollars very, very soon. And the amount of money hiring lobbyists and people who would engage in advertising and campaign contributions and all the rest is going to overwhelm our system, I am afraid, if we do not get this legislation passed this year.

So if we want to adopt good public policy, to prevent this kind of activity, to enforce the public policy of the States, it is important that we do it this year. I thank you, Mr. Chairman.

Mr. CHABOT. Thank you very much, Senator.

It is my understanding that the Senator has to catch a plane in a short time, so we are going to ask our questions at this time, before we hear the testimony of the other two panel members.

Mr. KYL. I appreciate that.

Mr. CHABOT. I will begin, and the first question, Senator, is why does the bill not apply to certain lawful regulated State gaming industries?

Mr. KYL. The bill would prohibit Internet gambling by anyone, including an entity currently involved in State lawful gaming activity. They would not be able to engage in Internet gambling operations.

Mr. SCOTT. Would the gentleman yield?

Mr. CHABOT. Yes, I will yield.

Mr. SCOTT. What did you mean by other than activities which are otherwise legal? What does that mean?

Mr. KYL. That means that we do not prohibit activities which States have determined to be legal, like their State lotteries, Indian gambling consistent with IGRA, the parimutuel wagering, and fantasy sports. Those are the four primary areas where activity is currently being engaged in, and that is lawful activity in those States. We do not prohibit that. But it is important to note that none of that activity involves Internet gambling the way it is identified in our legislation.

Mr. CHABOT. Reclaiming my time, Senator, Jay Cohen, an American citizen, was convicted last week under the Wire Act of operating an Internet sports betting business from Antigua. Senator, how does the Cohen case affect the continuing need for Federal legislation?

Mr. KYL. I applauded that conviction, but it is interesting that some others were not brought to trial because we could not gain physical jurisdiction over them because they had fled the jurisdiction. Most of the sites that are now transmitting these virtual casinos over the web are offshore sites, so it would not be possible to bring those people to justice in U.S. courts.

There is also a potential problem, and I do not want to overemphasize this because I support the Department of Justice's efforts to continue to bring prosecutions under the 1961 act. However, a clever defendant, I think, could mount a credible defense that if a signal is not transmitted over telephone or wire, it would not be covered by the terms of the Telephone or Wire Act. If it is by fiber optic cable or microwave satellite transmission, I think there may be a problem there, but I will leave that to the Department of Justice.

Mr. CHABOT. I am going to yield back the balance of my time at this time and I will yield to the gentleman from Virginia for 5 minutes.

Mr. SCOTT. Thank you, Mr. Chairman.

Senator, I am back to this "otherwise legal." The things that you said were legal now, am I understanding you, you can continue to do them? What does that have to do with the Internet?

Mr. KYL. Representative Scott, not much, except that in some cases, computers are used, networks are used. The furthest extension of the use of the Internet, I believe, today, and that which comes closest to what we would prohibit, are the so-called closed-loop subscriber-based systems. That would be the maximum permitted, and that is not a situation where anyone can just log on in their home and participate in a virtual casino. But if you are at a particular identifiable site and you are a subscriber to this particular system, you can log on and within a very closed loop, not the Internet generally—for example, if you are in, let us say, New Jersey, you might be able to bet on a race occurring in California if those two States have an agreement.

Mr. SCOTT. You said is otherwise lawful. If the State changes its laws and allows subscribers to subscribe to that closed loop, that would be legal?

Mr. KYL. Yes, it would.

Mr. SCOTT. So that kind of opens up a little loophole, because if you subscribe, you are in.

Mr. KYL. Representative Scott, it certainly would permit the use of the closed-loop subscriber system, but it would not violate the central tenet of this legislation, which is that if the person can log on in his or her own home and engage in this activity from wherever the signal might emanate. It would have to be at a physical site that the State identifies. It would have to be pursuant to the State regulatory commission signing off on the process, and it would have to be a particular agreement with another State for a closed-loop system, unless it was a purely intrastate situation.

Mr. SCOTT. If the Virginia lottery wanted to allow people in Virginia to buy lottery tickets over the Internet and we passed a bill in Virginia to allow that, what would happen?

Mr. KYL. If the State of Virginia wanted to let people log on their own home computer and participate in a State lottery, it would be prohibited under the Senate bill.

Mr. SCOTT. Does your bill contain a prohibition against individuals gambling on the Internet, or does it prohibit businesses from running a gambling operation only?

Mr. KYL. Technically, it is the latter, Representative Scott. We had originally drafted the legislation to provide a crime both for the bettor and the entity conducting the gambling. The Justice Department was concerned that that would put an undue burden on the Federal law enforcement agencies. In recognition of the fact that the States still have the option to prosecute under the State laws, we removed the crime for the individual bettor, and so it would be up to the individual States to enforce their laws against the individual bettor if they so choose.

Mr. SCOTT. You had indicated, I do not know if maybe we can get somebody else to answer this, but technologically, you indicated that you would have the ability to shut down a site when it crossed the United States borders. With the technology of the Internet, I have a feeling that that is going to be kind of difficult to do, particularly when you can use the telephone line to call a switchboard in another country to connect you with the site. It would be virtually impossible to ever get jurisdiction over such a thing and if you could ever figure out that the connection had been made to begin with.

Mr. KYL. Mr. Chairman and Representative Scott, that is an excellent question. What I said was really an oversimplification to amplify it just a little bit. It is not going to be technologically easy in all cases. That is point number one.

Point two, we are not confident that we can gain jurisdiction over the perpetrators and bring them to justice, so that is not the primary focus of the legislation. The primary focus is to stop the illegal activity from being conducted in the United States.

So then we get to the third point. How is that done? In most situations, it should be possible to prevent the signal from being transmitted throughout the United States by either asking the service provider to cease providing service to that site, or in the case of a switch, to filter out the particular signal coming through from that illegal website offshore. Because of the continuing evolution of the technology, this process will continue to evolve.

I have described it in layman's terms. Technologically, it is a lot more complicated than that, which is why we have in the legislation a provision that if the service provider or switching entity or other entity involved in stopping the service cannot technically do the job, or if it is too expensive for them to do it, relatively speaking, then, of course, they would not be required to do so.

So it is possible that there may be some situations in which it is hard, it takes time, or may even become impossible to stop the transmission. But as it stands right now, we believe that it would be possible to stop most of these transmissions.

Mr. SCOTT. Thank you, Mr. Chairman.

Mr. CHABOT. Thank you. I would ask unanimous consent to allow Mr. Goodlatte to ask questions if he chooses to do so. Without objection, it is so ordered.

Mr. GOODLATTE. Thank you, Mr. Chairman. I actually do not have any questions of the Senator. I just want to say that I appreciate his good work and look forward to continuing to work with him. There are a small number of differences between the legislation that I and Congressman LoBiondo have introduced in the House and the version you have in the Senate, but I am confident we can work out those differences and have one bill at the end of the day that could be signed into law.

Mr. KYL. Thank you very much, Representative Goodlatte. I look forward to working with you, Mr. Chairman, Representative Scott, and anybody else that has an interest in this. This is an activity which is very pernicious, particularly with regard to our kids, and I think it is time that we deal with it this year, as I said.

Mr. CHABOT. Thank you very much, Senator. We appreciate you being here this afternoon.

We will now hear from Mr. DiGregory, who has already been introduced, followed by Mr. Doyle, who has also been introduced, and then we will question these witnesses. Mr. DiGregory?

STATEMENT OF KEVIN V. DIGREGORY, DEPUTY ASSISTANT ATTORNEY GENERAL, CRIMINAL DIVISION, UNITED STATES DEPARTMENT OF JUSTICE

Mr. DIGREGORY. Thank you, Mr. Chairman, members of the subcommittee, for providing me this opportunity to provide you with the Department of Justice's views on Internet gambling and H.R. 3125, the Internet Gambling Prohibition Act of 1999.

The growing availability of emerging technologies has had a prolific effect on gambling. The Internet and other new technologies have made possible types of gambling that were not feasible a few years ago. For example, a U.S. citizen can now log on from his living room and participate in an interactive Internet poker game operated from a computer located in Antigua. Not only have the Internet and other new technologies brought gambling into the home, they have made it anonymous and readily available to virtually anyone at any time and at anyplace where there is an Internet hookup.

As a result, the number of Internet gambling sites operating illegal betting and wagering businesses online has increased at an alarmingly rapid rate. The Department is deeply troubled by this proliferation of gambling on the Internet for three reasons.

First, since the Internet allows virtually instantaneous and anonymous communication that is difficult to trace to a particular individual or organization. The potential for operators of Internet gambling sites to successfully defraud their customers is significantly greater than with traditional casino-style gambling. Fraudulent activities can range from credit card fraud to the manipulation of gambling odds.

Of course, and as the Deputy Attorney General noted before this same subcommittee on February 29, we recognize that there are legitimate reasons to allow anonymity in communications networks. A whistle blower or a member of a battered women's support group, for example, may understandably wish to use the Internet and other new technologies to communicate with others without revealing his or her identity. Nonetheless, such admittedly legitimate uses for anonymity on the Internet involve legal activities and are inapplicable in connection with gambling on the Internet, which is illegal.

Second, because the Internet provides people with virtually unfettered access to the opportunity to gamble at any time and from anyplace, Internet gambling presents a greater danger for compulsive gamblers and can cause severe financial consequences for an unsuccessful player.

Last, because the Internet is both anonymous and widely available, it is much more difficult to prevent minors from gambling. Currently, Internet gambling businesses have no reliable way of confirming that gamblers are not minors who have gained access to a credit card and are gambling on their websites.

Despite the proliferation of Internet gambling, the Department is optimistic about its ability to combat this form of illegal gambling. Just last week, as was earlier noted by Mr. Chabot, a jury in the Federal District Court in New York found Jay Cohen, the owner of an Internet gambling site in Antigua, guilty of violating 18 United States Code Section 1084, a statute that makes it illegal for a betting or wagering business to use a wire communication facility to transmit bets or wagers in interstate or foreign commerce.

Several of the counts for which Mr. Cohen was found guilty solely involved his Internet operations. This is not to say that Section 1084 as written will apply in every case. As I will explain later in my testimony, the Department believes that the statute may need to be amended to assist us in our efforts against gambling and organized crime.

Before I discuss that, however, let me say that the Department has reviewed H.R. 3125 and is very concerned about how it proposes to deal with Internet gambling. The Department is most concerned about the following three issues.

First, we are concerned that the bill does not really prohibit Internet gambling, but rather facilitates certain types of gambling from the home and, therefore, arguably expands gambling opportunities. Specifically, the Department notes that H.R. 3125 exempts parimutuel wagering from the prohibition against Internet gambling. The result is that people will be able to bet on horse racing, dog racing, and jai alai from their living rooms.

While the bill provides that such gambling must be done on a closed-loop subscriber-based service, we believe the definition of that term is extremely broad. I could receive, for example, a free disk in the mail, load it on my computer, connect through my regular Internet service provider, and start betting on horse racing from my living room. Additionally, if my children have access to that same computer, they may also be able to get online and bet and wager on parimutuel activities.

Simply stated, we do not understand why the parimutuel wagering industry should be allowed to accept bets from people in their homes when other forms of gambling have rightly been prohibited from doing so. The same concerns that we have expressed about children and compulsive gamblers having unfettered access to gambling via the Internet is true whether the betting is on horse races or on casino games.

Related to this point is our second concern, that the passing of H.R. 3125 will allow gambling online that currently is not allowed in the physical world. For example, people cannot currently legally call gambling businesses in other States from their homes and place bets on horse races. Yet, H.R. 3125 would allow them to place the same such bets over the Internet. It is hard for the Department to understand why conduct previously deemed unacceptable in the physical world and over the telephone should now be legal when carried out in cyberspace.

Third, we do not believe that H.R. 3125 is technology neutral but applies only to Internet gambling while leaving the existing prohibition on gambling over wire communication facilities in general unchanged. While the Department is concerned about legislation designed for particular technologies such as the Internet, it is specifically troubled here by the creation of two inconsistent gambling prohibitions, two inconsistent, as we see it from the perspective of the prosecutor, enforcement schemes, one expressly for the Internet and a different one for the use of wire communications facilities. And by the way, as was noted in the Cohen case, we believe that wire communications facilities, so long as you connect to the Internet over the wire, include the Internet.

Indeed, any effort to distinguish Internet transmission from other methods of communication is likely to create artificial and unworkable distinctions. For example, we expect that digital telephony will grow in popularity over the next few years. How would we deal with gambling that occurred over this technology, which would use the Internet or other packet-switched networks for pure voice communications? Would it be under the proposed Section 1085, which is designed specifically for the Internet, or would it be under Section 1084, which deals with wire communications in general but, as I mentioned earlier, also can include the Internet? This is especially problematic as Section 1084 and the new Section 1085 proposed by H.R. 3125 would have different standards and punishments.

The Department urges Congress to identify the conduct that it is trying to prohibit and then to prohibit that conduct in technology-neutral terms. The fact that gambling, an age-old crime, has gone high-tech and can now be done through the Internet is no reason to pass new laws that specifically target the Internet for regulation. Passing laws that are technology-specific can create overlapping and conflicting laws, prohibiting the same activity but with different legal standards and punishments.

This, we believe, will be the result if H.R. 3125 is enacted in its current form. We will have both Section 1084, which we have used to prosecute Internet gambling, and a new Section 1085, which would prohibit some, but not all, types of Internet gambling. This overlap in the statute can only complicate law enforcement's efforts on the Internet gambling front.

The Department encourages Congress, especially as it encounters more traditional crimes being committed online, to ensure that existing laws are sufficient and technology-neutral in their approach and that they do not single out the Internet for regulation. If you deem existing laws to be insufficient, then please consider legislation, whether it is prohibitive or permissive, which focuses on specific conduct and not on the specific medium employed to perpetrate that conduct.

One last problem that we perceive with H.R. 3125 is that we have identified the bill's silence on Indian gaming issues. The Department believes that any Internet gambling legislation should not appeal or amend the rights or privileges secured tribes under the Indian Gaming Regulatory Act. Of course, to the extent that Indian tribes seek to offer gaming to citizens of various States where such gaming does not take place solely on Indian lands and is not otherwise authorized by law, there is no compelling reason to exempt Indian tribes from the otherwise generally applicable provisions of the legislation for such off-reservation gambling.

For all of the reasons I have discussed, the Department urges Congress to amend existing gambling laws rather than to create a new technology-specific statutory scheme. As I noted earlier, Section 1084 criminalizes those betting and wagering businesses that transmit bets or wagers on sporting events or contests over the Internet. We recognize that Section 1084 was enacted almost 40 years ago and may need to be amended to bring it into the 21st century. We believe that it can be done effectively through the following actions.

First, amend Section 1084 so that it clearly applies to all betting and wagering and includes the transmission of bets or wagers over any communications facilities. Such an amendment would eliminate any doubt about whether 1084 applies only to bets or wagers on sporting events or contests. It would also ensure that future technologies that are not wire-based communications facilities are covered by Section 1084.

Second, add several definitions to 18 United States Code 1081. For example, we would recommend adding definitions for transmission, bets or wagers, and information assisting in the placing of bets or wagers.

Third, amend Section 1084 to specifically cover those individuals in the betting and wagering business who are located outside of the territorial jurisdiction of the United States when those individuals knowingly facilitate or aid in the unlawful betting and wagering by transmitting a better wager to or from an individual located within the United States. While the current statute does include those transmissions involving interstate and foreign commerce, it is unclear whether the statute would cover someone who, on a boat out in the middle of the Atlantic Ocean who is using a cellular phone to take bets or wagers, takes a bet from a citizen located perhaps in Miami or Cape Hatteras or New York City.

Requiring any person, not just a common carrier, that provides a facility to any individual in the business of betting and wagering to disconnect service when served with proper lawful process by law enforcement agencies. We would also extend the same protections against liability contained in the existing statute for common carriers to these persons. You may be aware that there is a section in 1084, Section 1084(d), which allows law enforcement, State, local, or Federal law enforcement, to go to a common carrier, advise the common carrier that an illegal gambling business is being operated or is about to be operated over that service, and the common carrier, once notified by law enforcement, can then either terminate or decide not to connect the service of the particular business which is about to be run or is being run.

Mr. CHABOT. Mr. DiGregory, if you could wrap up your testimony, we would appreciate it.

Mr. DIGREGORY. Fifth, clarify that Section 1084 does not repeal or amend the rights or privileges of tribes secured under IGRA.

Sixth, clarify that 1084 does not prohibit how States are currently legally using communication facilities in the operation of multi-State lotteries, like Powerball.

We believe that if 1084 is amended in these ways, many of our concerns, as well as the concerns that led to the introduction of these bills, would be addressed. We would be happy and privileged to work with you toward accomplishing this goal, and I want to thank you again for allowing me to be here today and present our views and I would be glad to answer, or at least try to answer, any questions you might have.

Mr. CHABOT. Thank you, Mr. DiGregory.

[The prepared statement of Mr. DiGregory follows:]

PREPARED STATEMENT OF KEVIN V. DIGREGORY, DEPUTY ASSISTANT ATTORNEY GENERAL, CRIMINAL DIVISION, UNITED STATES DEPARTMENT OF JUSTICE

Thank you, Mr. Chairman and Members of the Subcommittee, for providing me this opportunity to provide the Subcommittee with the Department of Justice's views on Internet gambling and H.R. 3125, the "Internet Gambling Prohibition Act of 1999."

The growing availability of emerging technologies has had a prolific effect on gambling. The Internet and other new technologies have made possible types of gambling that were not feasible a few years ago. For example, a U.S. citizen can now log on from his living room and participate in an interactive Internet poker game operated from a computer located in Antigua. Not only have the Internet and other new technologies brought gambling into the home, they have made it anonymous and readily available to virtually anyone at any time and at any place where there is an Internet hookup. As a result, the number of Internet gambling sites operating illegal betting and wagering businesses online has increased at an alarmingly rapid rate. The Department is deeply troubled by this proliferation of gambling on the Internet for three reasons.

First, since the Internet allows virtually instantaneous and anonymous communication that is difficult to trace to a particular individual or organization, the potential for operators of Internet gambling sites to successfully defraud their customers is significantly greater than with traditional casino-style gambling. Fraudulent activities can range from credit card fraud to the manipulation of gambling odds. Of course—and as the Deputy Attorney General noted before this Subcommittee on February 29th—we recognize that there are legitimate reasons to allow anonymity in communications networks. A whistleblower or a member of a battered woman's support group, for example, may understandably wish to use the Internet and other new technologies to communicate with others without revealing his or her identify. Nonetheless, such admittedly legitimate uses for anonymity on the Internet involve *legal* activities and are inapplicable in connection with gambling on the Internet, which is *illegal*.

Second, because the Internet provides people with virtually unfettered access to the opportunity to gamble at any time and from any place, Internet gaming presents a greater danger for compulsive gamblers and can cause severe financial consequences for an unsuccessful player.

Last, because the Internet is both anonymous and widely available, it is much more difficult to prevent minors from gambling. Currently, Internet gambling businesses have no reliable way of confirming that gamblers are not minors who have gained access to a credit card and are gambling on their web sites.

Despite the proliferation of Internet gambling, the Department is optimistic about its ability to combat this form of illegal gambling. Just last week, a jury in federal district court in New York found Jay Cohen, the owner of an Internet gambling site in Antigua, guilty of violating 18 U.S.C. § 1084, a statute that makes it illegal for a betting or wagering business to use a wire communication facility to transmit bets or wagers in interstate or foreign commerce. Several of the counts for which Mr. Cohen was found guilty solely involved his Internet operations. That is not to say that section 1084, as written, will apply in every case. As I will explain later in my testimony, the Department believes that the statute may need to be amended to assist us in our efforts against gambling and organized crime.

Before I discuss that, however, let me say that the Department has reviewed H.R. 3125 in great detail and is very concerned about how it proposes to deal with Internet gambling. The Department is most concerned about the following three issues.

First, the Department is concerned that the bill does not really prohibit Internet gambling, but rather facilitates certain types of gambling from the home and, therefore, arguably expands gambling opportunities. Specifically, the Department recognizes that H.R. 3125 exempts parimutuel wagering from the prohibition against Internet gambling. The result is that people will be able to bet on horse racing, dog racing, and jai alai from their living rooms. While the bill provides that such gambling must be done on a "closed loop subscriber based service," the definition of that term is extremely broad. I could receive a free disk in the mail, load it on my computer, connect through my regular Internet service provider, and start betting on horse racing from my living room. Additionally, if my children have access to that same computer, they may also be able to get online and bet and wager on parimutuel activities.

Simply stated, the Department does not understand why the parimutuel wagering industry should be allowed to accept bets from people in their homes, when other forms of gambling have rightly been prohibited from doing so. The same concerns that we have expressed about children and compulsive gamblers having unfettered access to gambling via the Internet is true whether the betting is on horse races or on casino games.

Related to this point is the Department's second concern that the passing of H.R. 3125 will allow gambling online that currently is not allowed in the physical world. For example, people cannot not currently legally call gambling businesses in others states from their homes and place bets on horse races. Yet, H.R. 3125 would allow them to place the same such bets over the Internet. It is hard for the Department to understand why conduct previously deemed unacceptable in the physical world and over the telephone should now be legal when carried out in cyberspace.

Third, H.R. 3125 is not technology-neutral, but applies only to Internet gambling while leaving the existing prohibition on gambling over "wire communication facilities" in general unchanged. While the Department is generally concerned about legislation designed for particular technologies such as the Internet, it is specifically troubled here by the creation of two inconsistent gambling prohibitions—one expressly for the Internet and a different one for the use of wire communication facilities (which includes the Internet).

Indeed, any effort to distinguish Internet transmission from other methods of communication is likely to create artificial and unworkable distinctions. For example, we expect digital Internet telephony to grow in popularity over the next few years. How would we deal with gambling that occurred over this technology, which would use the Internet or other packet-switched networks for pure voice communications? Would it be under the proposed section 1085, which is designed specifically for the Internet, or under section 1084, which deals with wire communications in general (but also includes the Internet)? This is especially problematic, as section 1084 and the new section 1085 proposed by H.R. 3125 would have different standards and punishments.

The Department urges Congress to identify the conduct that it is trying to prohibit and then to prohibit that conduct in technology-neutral terms. The fact that gambling, an age-old crime, has gone high-tech and can now be done through the Internet, is no reason to pass new laws that specifically target the Internet for regulation. Passing laws that are technology-specific can create overlapping and conflicting laws prohibiting the same activity, but with different legal standards and punishments. This will be the result if H.R. 3125 is enacted in its current form. We will have both section 1084, which we've used to prosecute Internet gambling, and a new section 1085 which would prohibit some, but not all, types of Internet gambling. This overlap in the statutes can only complicate law enforcement's efforts on the Internet gambling front.

The Department encourages Congress, especially as it encounters more traditional crimes online, to ensure that existing laws are sufficient and technology-neutral in their approach and do not single out the Internet for regulation. If existing laws are deemed insufficient, please consider legislation, whether prohibitive or permissive, which focuses on specific conduct and not on the specific medium employed to perpetrate that conduct.

One last problem with H.R. 3125 that the Department has identified involves the bill's silence on Indian gaming issues. The Department believes that any Internet gambling legislation should not repeal or amend the rights or privileges secured tribes under IGRA. Of course, to the extent that Indian Tribes seek to offer gaming to citizens of various states, where such gaming does not take place solely on Indian lands and is not otherwise authorized by law, there is no compelling reason to exempt Indian Tribes from the otherwise generally applicable provisions of the legislation for such off-reservation gambling.

For all of the reasons I've discussed, the Department urges Congress to amend existing gambling laws, rather than create a new technology-specific statutory scheme.

As I noted earlier, section 1084 criminalizes those betting and wagering businesses that transmit bets or wagers on sporting events or contests over the Internet. The Department recognizes, however, that section 1084, which was enacted almost forty years ago, may need to be amended to bring it into the 21st Century. The Department believes that this can be done through the following actions:

(1) Amending section 1084 so that it clearly applies to all betting or wagering and includes the transmission of bets or wagers over any communications facilities. Such an amendment would eliminate any doubt about whether section 1084 only applies to bets or wagers on sporting events and contests. It would also ensure that future technologies that are not wire-based communication facilities are covered by section 1084.

(2) Adding several definitions to 18 U.S.C. § 1081. For example, we would recommend adding the following definitions for "transmission," "bets or wagers," and "information assisting in the placing of bets or wagers."

(3) Amending section 1084 to specifically cover those individuals in the betting and wagering business who are located outside the territorial jurisdiction of the United States, when those individuals knowingly facilitate or aid in unlawful betting and wagering by transmitting a bet or wager to or from an individual located within the United States. While the current statute includes those transmissions involving interstate and foreign commerce, it is unclear whether the statute would cover someone on a boat in the middle of the Atlantic Ocean who is using a cellular phone to take bets or wagers from a U.S. citizen located in Miami.

(4) Requiring any person, not just a common carrier, that provides a facility to an individual in the business of betting and wagering to disconnect service when served with proper lawful process by law enforcement agencies. We would also extend the same protections against liability contained in the existing statute for common carriers to these persons.

(5) Clarifying that section 1084 does not repeal or amend the rights or privileges secured tribes under IGRA.

(6) Clarifying that section 1084 does not prohibit how states are currently legally using communication facilities in the operation of multi-state lotteries.

The Department of Justice believes that if 1084 were to be amended in these ways, many of our concerns, as well as the concerns that led to the introduction of Internet gambling bills, would be addressed. We would be happy to work with Congress towards this goal.

I want to thank the Subcommittee again for asking me to present the Department's views on Internet gambling. I would now be pleased to answer any questions you may have.

Mr. CHABOT. Mr. Doyle?

STATEMENT OF JAMES E. DOYLE, ATTORNEY GENERAL, STATE OF WISCONSIN, MADISON, WI

Mr. DOYLE. Thank you, Mr. Chairman. I want to express the thanks not only personally but on behalf of the National Association of Attorneys General for this hearing, for the opportunity to be heard. We want to thank Representative Goodlatte for his work on this. We have worked very closely with Senator Kyl over the years.

When we started out on this, a committee of State Attorneys General, which at time—I guess it shows you the time that has passed—consisted of myself, Dan Lundgren of California, and Skip Humphrey of Minnesota. I am the only one left in the association since we started. That was the committee, and we were looking at Internet crime, and we looked at a variety—this was back in 1994, as it was just starting to happen. One of the areas that we certainly identified was the problem of gambling.

We did what I believe was the first report nationally on the extent of Internet gambling at the time, and we were concerned because we located, as Senator Kyl indicated, about 23 online gambling sites. We at that time expressed concern that this was going to grow into a billion-dollar business with hundreds of sites. Well, here we are 5 years later with hundreds of sites, I guess it is estimated to be 700 sites, and no real end to this growth in sight.

In addition, we are still seeing only the beginning of Internet gambling. With the increased band widths, with DSLs, with increased modem speeds, people will not be playing blackjack on the Internet. Within the next couple of years, every home computer will be a gambling machine with the cherries spinning on the screen and that kind of fast action, fast-paced gambling right in people's homes. Most experts on gambling will say that that is the most addictive kind of gambling. It is something we regulate very closely at the State level, and yet it will be available to everybody in their homes in a very short period of time.

So even what we are seeing today, I think most people who look at this recognize is still just the beginning of what is going to be a multi-multi-billion-dollar enterprise that will make the typical casinos and so on that we have in the United States be relatively insignificant.

Now, there are longstanding State policies, and there has been a lot of discussion here today, and to me, this is really the heart of it. We have over the decades and centuries, in fact, left to the States the decision on what will be the scope of gambling within their States, and in the United States today, we range from Nevada with relatively universal gambling to the States of Utah and Hawaii, which to date still allow no legal gambling at all. Those are decisions that we leave to the States and we should not permit the growth of the Internet to take away from the States that authority, that sovereignty to make those decisions.

In the State of Wisconsin, the prohibition against gambling was included in our first State constitution in 1848. It has been amended several times since then by the voters of the State. As recently as 1994, the voters of our State amended our constitution to make it clear that we only wanted the State lottery and parimutuel dog or horse racing in the State. We specifically constitutionally prohibited video gambling machines, which is what home computers are rapidly becoming. We made that decision as a State in our constitution and that is why we are here asking Congress for help.

I will tell you, in Wisconsin, I cannot speak for other States, but we do not want commercial gambling reaching into the homes of our States. We have no way to regulate that gambling. I have often thought that playing poker, or so-called poker over the Internet is like playing it over the telephone, where the other side gets to see your hand, and when you show your hand you say, well, I have got a full house and the other side says, sorry, I have got four aces, and you have to accept the findings. That is what Internet gambling is.

We tightly regulate in Wisconsin the State lottery, the dog tracks. We were the first State in the country to enter into compacts with all of our Indian tribes which call for joint regulation between the tribes and the States. We regulate tightly the gambling that goes on in the State of Wisconsin.

We also are highly concerned about the addiction problems of gambling. We are already seeing it at casinos in the State and other forms of gambling. But the thought, as we heard testimony here today, of an individual just who can turn on the computer in his home at any time and engage in gambling removes the kinds of barriers that we have had.

We had testimony today from somebody who had a father who could apparently give him a credit card and float $5,000 loans. The kind of addicted gamblers we see do not have that kind of backup for their addiction and we see very serious problems that come with people who do not have fathers handing them credit cards, with all due respect to Mr. Doe, but instead have nothing and are in terrible financial straits after this happens.

And we are obviously in Wisconsin very concerned about the access of young people to gambling. They do not get into the Indian casinos in our State. They are not permitted. They are checked at the point of purchasing a lottery ticket. They do not place bets at the dog track. And yet, they are able to gamble on the Internet.

Now, we are here in a very unusual position as State Attorneys General. We are here asking Congress to act. Normally, we are here saying, we will take care of our own problems and we do not want you to act. We think you have federalized crime too much. But here, we are saying that this is truly an instance where the exercise of Federal power, in fact, furthers State sovereignty, where the exercise of Federal power creates the climate by which we can seek to determine our own course in our own States with respect to the extent of gambling that we want.

There has been discussion about the horse racing, the parimutuel exemption and so on. Certainly, and Senator Kyl and Representative Goodlatte and others have worked very hard on this, but the underlying principle of those provisions is to make sure that States can make their own choices about what the extent of parimutuel betting will be. This is not unfettered parimutuel betting. The drafts, the proposals, the bills have attempted to make it clear that States can make their own choices.

So again, I appreciate the committee's willingness to listen to us, to work with me and with the other members of the association. We as an association strongly believe this because we see this as a States' rights issue. We see this as a way for the proper exercise of Federal jurisdiction to permit States to make their own very basic judgments about policy within the States. Thank you.

Mr. CHABOT. Thank you very much, Mr. Doyle.

[The prepared statement of Mr. Doyle follows:]

PREPARED STATEMENT OF JAMES E. DOYLE, ATTORNEY GENERAL, STATE OF WISCONSIN, MADISON, WI

Good afternoon.

I appreciate the opportunity to appear today before the Subcommittee on this important issue.

State Attorneys General have been working on the serious law enforcement issues posed by Internet gambling since 1995. We have always seen this issue as one that presents unique problems for state law enforcement officials.

Though we traditionally urge Congress to preserve state-level decision-making on most criminal justice issues, we have asked the federal government to expand its law enforcement role in the area of Internet gambling. Our concerns have led the National Association of Attorneys General to seek federal legislation to implement a uniform federal prohibition against the use of the Internet and related computer networks for gambling purposes.

Gambling has always been a state issue. It is mentioned, and generally prohibited, in nearly every state constitution. State gambling policies and laws differ more widely than in almost any other area of the law. From complete gambling prohibitions in Utah and Hawaii to the huge commercial casinos of Nevada, Atlantic City and the Mississippi Gulf Coast, each state has chosen to draw the line on gambling based on local and state interests. In my own state, the gambling policy is part of our state constitution. Expanding gambling in Wisconsin requires not only the approval of our state legislature, but the approval of the voters in a statewide referendum.

The Internet threatens to disrupt each state's carefully crafted choice on gambling policy. By using technology and the tools of electronic commerce, a person no longer needs to get on a plane to Las Vegas to gamble in a large casino. Instead, they can simply log on to the Internet from their home or office and bet on any event imaginable, or play exciting and colorful interactive casino games that offer real money as prizes. Technologically, it doesn't matter that the person's home state has chosen to prohibit this potentially harmful activity, because the Internet crosses jurisdictional boundaries and has the potential to make any online activity available to anybody, anywhere, at any time.

It is important to remember that the Internet has provided, and will continue to provide, wonderful benefits to our society. It has brought the tools of the information age into the lives of millions of people who would otherwise not have access to such resources. It empowers people by giving them the information they need to make educated choices in their lives via their home, office or a public library computer. The Internet gives us access to medical, educational and cultural resources from around the world.

But the Internet's ability to cross boundaries and make technological advances available to everybody has also presented some of the problems addressed by the proposed Internet Gambling Prohibition Act. Without attempting to reach out and tackle these issues, individual state laws will have an uneven and minimal effect on the growth of this industry as a whole.

There is really no question that states can legally and constitutionally exercise criminal or civil jurisdiction over out-of-state gambling operators who project those businesses into their states. My office has brought several successful lawsuits against Internet gambling operations that violated Wisconsin law. But practical problems, such as difficulties with international extradition and the wide disparity of available enforcement resources, prevent uniform application of state laws, and allow an illegal enterprise to operate essentially unchecked throughout this country. No individual state could effectively address the more than 700 Internet gambling sites on the World Wide Web today, or even a significant proportion of them. Gambling on the Internet is much like the Wild Wild West, and foreign jurisdictions have become the hideouts for the bandits.

Federal legislation, like that being considered by this Subcommittee, can help combat this activity. In spite of its continued illegality, the vast majority of the world's Internet gambling players are right here in the United States. The reach of the federal courts goes well beyond each state's borders. The tools for injunctive relief provide much-needed preventative measures. The clarification of the criminal measures provides real penalties for the businesses taking advantage of the vacuum in the current wire act—a vacuum created by new technologies and their ability to allow new forms of gambling to occur over the wires.

Senator Jon Kyl has worked closely with my office and the National Association of Attorneys General for several years on this issue. His efforts resulted in the passage, by unanimous consent, of the Senate version of the Internet Gambling Prohibition Act. After working closely with all of the parties affected by this legislation, he has been able to craft a bill which generally prohibits at-home gambling, while allowing existing licensed and regulated gambling enterprises to utilize technology to continue operating their own businesses. The strength of Senator Kyl's bill is that it allows states to continue to make their own decisions on what is legal and acceptable within their own borders, honoring their state laws and regulatory structures, while providing a complete prohibition on at-home gambling via the Internet. This is something that no individual state's law could assure.

This Subcommittee is considering a bill that is similar in many important respects to the one already passed by the Senate. Hopefully, with continued effort by the proponents of this legislation, a final bill will be crafted which meets the needs of both bodies, and the bill can finally become law. I would like to point out the few distinctions between the House and Senate bills that raise concerns.

The most significant distinction from our perspective as state Attorneys General is the omission, perhaps merely by drafting oversight, of a clause assuring the applicability of other state and federal criminal laws to Internet gambling. The Senate bill provides in its "Rules of Construction" section that nothing in the prohibition section "may be construed to create immunity from criminal prosecution under any provision of Federal or State law." This language is very important in accomplishing the main goal of the bill, which is to bolster the ability of the individual states to fight this form of illegal gambling as it crosses their borders via the Internet. I would strongly urge the members to insert such language into the House version of this bill before its final passage.

Assuring the applicability of state criminal laws is especially important when I view another section which seems to allow for at-home sales of state lottery tickets via the Internet. This practice is currently illegal in most states, including my own, where such practice is prohibited by the state constitution. However, the language allowing state lotteries and their agents to sell tickets via "closed loop subscriber-based systems" protected only by a "user name and password" would seem to encourage this specific practice. At-home sales of gambling products should not be encouraged in any way by this legislation. The danger of such sales can be seen in the tendency of many to purchase tickets well beyond their means. It is especially timely to note this fact in light of the frenzy surrounding sales of lottery tickets just last week as the multi-state Powerball jackpot approached record levels.

I am also concerned with the blanket exception in the House bill for "any otherwise lawful bet or wager" made on the Internet, either intrastate or state-to-state. No such exception appears in the Senate bill. This section would exempt these "otherwise lawful" bets and wagers from this act, essentially throwing this issue back to a state-by-state analysis. While intended to allow each state some degree of autonomy, this provision instead opens the door to a new hodgepodge of Internet gambling laws in this country. "Otherwise lawful" is a term that can be interpreted many ways depending upon what a particular party is pushing, and its presence in federal law could dilute the clear policy statement this legislation could otherwise make.

Finally, I think it is important to address the issue of gambling on Indian lands more fully. The House bill's current reference to the Indian Gaming Regulatory Act and tribal-state compacts should be enough to prevent illegal Internet gambling, because those documents clearly limit Indian gaming activity to those activities and participants physically located on Indian lands. However, that view is not shared by all. Senator Campbell proposed extensive language to address the Indian gaming issue directly, and that language was inserted into the Senate bill by a floor amendment. It represents a strong attempt to clarify the needs of those involved in this complex and often contentious issue. I recommend that this body also adopt similar language to clarify for all involved the types of gaming that can be conducted utilizing the new technology of the Internet.

I want to thank the Subcommittee for inviting me to testify today. All of the amazing benefits of the Internet could come crashing down upon us if we do not make serious efforts, like those reflected in this bill, to prevent online gambling from running roughshod over state laws. The wire act is just not doing the job in preventing the wide variety of gambling activities available on the Internet. This is one of those unique situations where a federal prohibition will actually assure the continuation of states' abilities to control what occurs within their own borders.

Mr. CHABOT. Each panel member will now have 5 minutes to ask questions, and I will ask you the first question, Mr. Doyle. How do you respond to the assertion that States are seeking this type of legislation in order to protect their own revenues derived from gambling in their States, such as State lottery revenues? Would you respond, please?

Mr. DOYLE. Well, I hear that often argued, and the logical argument is that States, therefore, if they have a lottery, should open up all forms of gambling. I mean, there is no reason that gambling over the Internet is the one way that attacks the revenues of the State lottery. Apparently the argument is, if we have a State lottery, so that we are not looking like we are protecting the lottery, we should permit people to gamble in all forms so that the States cannot raise the revenue.

Obviously, lotteries came into place as a way for States to raise money, and as in Wisconsin, we only permit the State, except for dog track parimutuel licensed by the State, we only permit the State to gamble. That is true as far as letting bookies operate in our State. It is true as far as letting gambling go on over the Internet. We, by constitution, only permit the State to run a gambling operation in Wisconsin, with the one exception of parimutuel dog track or race track, highly licensed and highly regulated by the State.

Mr. CHABOT. Thank you. Some have said that gambling on the Internet cannot be effectively prohibited, so it should instead be regulated and revenues derived from it. Do you have a response to that?

Mr. DOYLE. Well, I have two responses, I guess. One is, they ought to go make those arguments in the 50 States of the United States who have the real decision to decide how much gambling. There is a legitimate argument that goes on in all of our States between people who are in favor of permitting gambling with regulation and taxation, as opposed to people who would seek to prohibit all of gambling. That is the fundamental question. That is the question that has to be argued out in State legislatures and not in the national Congress. I do not believe the national Congress should be deciding that fundamental question about whether we should prohibit or we should regulate and tax.

If I could also say, because there has been a good deal of discussion about whether you can actually prohibit all of Internet gambling, obviously, you cannot. You know, I have been in law enforcement much of my career. There are a lot of laws on the books which have not been 100 percent successful in reducing that kind of activity. Gambling is among them. I have spent years as a local prosecutor with prosecutions against bookies and others.

However, I believe that a Federal law that prohibits it and does give the kind of enforcement mechanism that permits not only the Federal Government but the State Attorneys General to go to Federal courts to get injunctions prohibiting this kind of gambling will sharply reduce the growth and the proliferation of this kind of gambling in the United States.

Mr. CHABOT. And how do you respond to the Department of Justice's claim that this legislation would in some way facilitate in-home Internet gambling instead of accomplishing its intended purposes to ban gambling over the Internet?

Mr. DOYLE. Well, with all due respect to my friend, Mr. DiGregory, I think that if the State decides that it wants to have parimutuel betting and it wants to have a closed loop that does not permit others in and closes that loop in some way, that a State should be able to make that decision.

I will tell you, in my State, I would be opposed to that kind of legislation, but I think a State should make that decision. And contrary to his comments, I do not see that this legislation in any way opens the door for further gambling other than what States specifically permit.

Mr. CHABOT. Thank you. Mr. DiGregory, does the Indian Gaming Regulatory Act authorize gaming beyond Indian lands?

Mr. DIGREGORY. No, it does not.

Mr. CHABOT. Does that mean that a bettor must be physically present on the Indian lands for the bet to be lawful under the IGRA?

Mr. DIGREGORY. That is what we believe it to mean, Mr. Chabot, and in fact, there was a recent case that involved the Coeur d'Alene tribe in Idaho where the Coeur d'Alene tribe wanted to offer a lottery, both over the telephone and over the Internet. I believe 13 State Attorneys General challenged the offering of that lottery and basically used 1084(d) and went to AT&T and asked AT&T not to provide service.

The position taken by AT&T in not providing service was upheld by the District Court in Idaho, and a further point that was made by the District Court was that the Indian Gaming Regulatory Act does require that the gaming be conducted on Indian lands, and if you were going to allow someone from, for example, the District of Columbia to telephone in a bet to the Coeur d'Alene reservation in Idaho, that that would not be in conformity with the Indian Gaming Regulatory Act because part of the game was being played in the District of Columbia.

Mr. CHABOT. Thank you. I see that I am out of time, so I am going to yield at this time to Mr. Scott.

Mr. SCOTT. Thank you, Mr. Chairman.

Mr. DiGregory, what is the present Federal law on horse race betting on the Internet and what would be the law after this bill passes?

Mr. DIGREGORY. Presently, because horse racing and betting on horse racing is sports betting, we believe that it violates Federal law for a gambling business to accept bets or wagers over a wire communication facility from another State.

Mr. SCOTT. What would be the law if this bill passes?

Mr. DIGREGORY. If this bill passes, we believe that the scheme would change, or another scheme would be in effect. If you used the closed-loop subscriber system, which we believe is very broad and would encompass using the Internet to place a bet, then someone could, apparently from their homes, make a bet interstate on a horse race, bet from, let us say, the District of Columbia on a horse race that is going on in another jurisdiction, or from—let us use Maryland—from Maryland to another jurisdiction where the race is being run.

Mr. SCOTT. Mr. Doyle, do you see the bill in its present form as an opportunity to expand betting?

Mr. DOYLE. No, I do not at all. In fact, I see the bill in its present form—there are some distinctions between the House and the Senate bill, but I see it as a way to try to restrict the amount of Internet gambling by unregulated sites. And if I might just say——

Mr. SCOTT. You keep talking about these unregulated sites. I have heard that a couple of times. What is a regulated site?

Mr. DOYLE. Well, I was about to mention the connection with the horse racing. What you are talking about is an operation highly regulated by—now, we do not have horse racing in Wisconsin, but we do have dogs—it is highly regulated. The government is very much involved in how the bets are played and auditing the books and so on. I also think there is a real——

Mr. SCOTT. And, therefore, you ought to be able to bet on dogs over the Internet?

Mr. DOYLE. If the State of Wisconsin makes that decision and it is a closed—now, I understand there are definitional issues, but it is a closed loop on a subscriber basis that does not allow somebody to just randomly log on and place that bet, I believe that is a decision for the State of Wisconsin.

I also believe there is a very significant constitutional issue that Mr. DiGregory's argument—we do not need to argue a Supreme Court case here, but we may someday, that if the State of Illinois and the State of Wisconsin decided both to have a horse racing operation, that they were going to have a closed-loop subscriber system and it is permitted and regulated by State law, I think there is a very significant Federal issue about whether 1084 can tell the State of Wisconsin and the State of Illinois not to enter into that compact. Now, we do not have that compact, but——

Mr. SCOTT. Let us talk about Powerball.

Mr. DOYLE. Powerball is permitted.

Mr. SCOTT. Okay.

Mr. DOYLE. We are part of compacts with Powerball. We have entered into compacts with other States for Powerball.

Mr. SCOTT. Technologically, Mr. DiGregory, how would you try to enforce the law as the bill is drafted without the personal liability on the gambler for a site that is physically operating out of a rogue country?

Mr. DIGREGORY. As H.R. 3125 is drafted, as I understand it, we could utilize a notice provision that is similar to the provision in 1084(d), and you could also utilize an injunction——

Mr. SCOTT. A notice to who?

Mr. DIGREGORY. A notice to the Internet service provider who is using or transmitting the site, even if the website is based overseas. There is injunctive relief, as well, that could be used.

Mr. SCOTT. And so how would you——

Mr. DIGREGORY. But that does not mean you are going to get personal jurisdiction over the person operating the site.

Mr. SCOTT. If you have got a site operating out of Iraq, who do you call to shut it down?

Mr. DIGREGORY. It depends on whether or not the site being operated out of Iraq is being carried by an Internet Service provider in this country. Then you could go to that Internet service provider in this country and seek injunctive relief or provide——

Mr. SCOTT. Name a provider. Are you talking about AOL? I mean, is that who you are talking about?

Mr. DIGREGORY. AOL is an Internet service provider, sure. There are lots of others.

Mr. SCOTT. So if the service is not being provided by someone—I mean, AOL is right here in Virginia.

Mr. DIGREGORY. Right.

Mr. SCOTT. You can talk to them. But suppose you have got an Internet service provider that is not located in the United States——

Mr. DIGREGORY. If you cannot get jurisdiction over somebody——

Mr. SCOTT [continuing]. Like Iraq.

Mr. DIGREGORY. If you cannot get jurisdiction over them, then you cannot give them the notice or you cannot get an injunction against them, or you can get an injunction against them but it is difficult to enforce.

Mr. SCOTT. And without personal liability on the part of the gambler, nothing happens.

Mr. DIGREGORY. That is a possible scenario, yes, sir.

Mr. SCOTT. And then the question we are addressed with is whether or not that is a better situation or a worse situation than just allowing it and regulating it.

Mr. DIGREGORY. Well, the point that Attorney General Doyle made earlier was even though we may not, if we seek to prohibit Internet gambling, be able to prohibit or prevent all Internet gambling from occurring, it still is a worthwhile exercise to try to gain control over this.

Mr. SCOTT. Mr. Chairman, I thank you for your indulgence. I think it puts us in a situation where we shut down everybody that could possibly be running a legitimate operation and giving an exclusive franchise to those who we have no jurisdiction over. Thank you for your indulgence.

Mr. CHABOT. We thank you for your questions, and I would also ask unanimous consent, once again, for Mr. Goodlatte to question witnesses. Without objection, we will defer to Mr. Goodlatte at this time.

Mr. GOODLATTE. Thank you, Mr. Chairman.

Mr. DiGregory, the Justice Department, as you clearly outlined, believes that there needs to be legislation to strengthen the current laws to deal with this issue, and in point of fact, Section 1084 is technology-specific to some extent, so it is not unique for section

1085 to also be technology-specific. Section 1084 does not prohibit you from traveling to Las Vegas or Atlantic City and placing a bet, even though you must cross interstate lines to do that.

Mr. DiGregory. That is right.

Mr. Goodlatte. The issue of being able to enforce this with regard to the individual gambler that Mr. Scott is concerned about, and as I indicated to Mr. Scott earlier, I share that concern. The legislation as originally drafted included that. As Senator Kyl pointed out, it was removed because of concern by the Justice Department that the Federal role in this would become overloaded. Nonetheless, States do have provisions in their law that prohibit individuals from participating in gambling within the State. Now, that individual is, in point of fact, not out of reach of the arm of Mr. Doyle in Wisconsin and other folks.

Mr. DiGregory. That is right.

Mr. Goodlatte. So if the State wants to prosecute that individual under State laws, they can do so right now, is that correct?

Mr. DiGregory. That is right, and, in fact, my prior experience as a prosecutor, I was in two different jurisdictions. I was in the Commonwealth of Pennsylvania and I was in the State of Florida, and those jurisdictions treated end betters differently. Now, do not ask me to remember which did which because it was too long ago for me to remember, but they treated end betters differently.

Mr. Goodlatte. Let me ask you this. How many Internet gambling websites exist right now? I think we have testimony that there are several hundred.

Mr. DiGregory. I agree with that. I think I have seen numbers like over 600.

Mr. Goodlatte. Do you know how many website operators have been indicted?

Mr. DiGregory. I know that Jay Cohen has been indicted. I know that there has also been an indictment and some guilty pleas in the Western District of Missouri—excuse me, did I say Western? Eastern District of Missouri.

Mr. Goodlatte. In the 2 years in which the industry has seen explosive growth in both sites and revenue, why has the Department not been more aggressive in pursuing those site operators which are clearly breaking the law?

Mr. DiGregory. Well, I think the Department has been aggressive. I think that one of the ways you are aggressive is by going after a provider like Mr. Cohen in a district where his operation and any publicity attendant to a crackdown on that operation is very visible. You are in a very high-profile media outlet where you will hopefully have the impact of deterring others from engaging in the same kind of business that Mr. Cohen has engaged in. There has, as I said, also been an effort in the Eastern District of Missouri against operators, and although I cannot go into detail, I know of other investigations that are ongoing as I sit here.

Mr. Goodlatte. Just to make one point of clarification, I picked up in your testimony that you felt that this bill allowed Indian gaming on the Internet. I want to make it clear that the legislation that I have introduced, H.R. 3125, has no exemption for Indian gaming on the Internet. Senator Kyl's legislation is different in that respect. It does allow, but it is only, to my knowledge, closed-loop as described by Mr. Doyle and only on the reservation, just as actions within a State would be the province of a State to be involved with.

Would you say it is a fair characterization of the different approach that I take and Senator Kyl takes as opposed to the approach that you take and the Justice Department takes in not trying to crack down on gambling on the Internet, which we both want to do, but in terms of having a respect for those State laws that Attorney General Doyle characterized in his testimony, and, for example, saying that if the State of Florida wants to allow somebody to place a bet on horse racing within the State of Florida from their home, the State should have the right to do that, that that is simply within the jurisdiction and the determination of the State, and that same situation would exist if the State of Illinois and the State of Wisconsin, as he described, wanted to have that relationship. That would be a determination of each of those States. They would both have to agree to do that before it would be lawful to do that under the law, and that is very similar to what takes place right now with regard to Powerball.

So the approach here is that yours would maintain the decision making process as to who can gamble and who cannot entirely at the Federal level, whereas ours would recognize that this technology has some interplay with currently existing State laws and that we are attempting to recognize the rights of those States to enforce those laws as they currently exist, modified by this new technological reality. Is that a fair distinction between my approach and yours?

Mr. DIGREGORY. I think that is one argument that can be made, yes.

Mr. GOODLATTE. Thank you.

Mr. DIGREGORY. But there are others, and one of the concerns that we have is, as I mentioned earlier, that horse racing on the Internet will be treated differently than it is now currently over the telephone. The current scheme with respect to horse racing over the telephone does recognize States' abilities to take bets on horse races. In fact, it recognizes the ability of States to take bets on horse races that are occurring outside their jurisdiction. What it does, however, is restrict the bet to a bet that is being placed intrastate with a State regulated industry, let us say within New York State, on a race that is going on in California or Oregon or wherever. I am not familiar with all of the States that have horse racing. Let us say Florida. I am familiar with Florida.

What it does not permit, though, it does not permit—the Interstate Horse Racing Act does not permit the transmission of an actual bet or wager by an individual sitting in New York on a horse race that is occurring in Florida. And as I said, one of the points that I tried to make earlier was——

Mr. GOODLATTE. Let me ask you how many prosecutions have occurred under that act.

Mr. DIGREGORY. I do not know how many prosecutions have occurred under that act.

Mr. GOODLATTE. I am not aware of any, are you?

Mr. DIGREGORY. I do not know of any prosecutions that have occurred under the act.

Mr. GOODLATTE. Would you be able to check on that— —

Mr. DIGREGORY. I would be glad to do it.

Mr. GOODLATTE [continuing]. And advise me of any actions taken under that provision of the existing law?

Mr. DIGREGORY. I am glad to do it.

Mr. GOODLATTE. Thank you. I thank the chairman.

Mr. CHABOT. Thank you. The gentleman's time has expired.

The gentlelady from Texas is recognized for 5 minutes.

Ms. JACKSON LEE. Thank you very much, Mr. Chairman. I thank the witnesses and the previous witnesses and appreciate their patience with my line of questioning, as much as I was detained in another hearing. But I do want to pursue both gentlemen and particularly the line of questioning of my colleague just a while back.

Mr. Doyle, as a State Attorney General, how do you find the efforts in terms of both legislative initiatives comporting with what you need to do on this issue of Internet gambling as it relates to Federal law versus State law? I assume that even if you did not speak to that, that you could help me understand what that does to what your efforts are attempting to do.

Mr. DOYLE. Yes. I believe that both of the bills greatly help States enforce their own State laws. I had indicated earlier that I think what these bills do is—it is the correct exercise of Federal jurisdiction by which you enhance the ability of States to enforce their own laws and to set their own gambling policy.

We have limited gambling in Wisconsin and we do not want 700, or soon to be whatever, 1,500 Internet gambling sites available to our children in our homes. This bill helps us to protect our own State policy with respect to gambling.

Ms. JACKSON LEE. One of the things I did not do is to thank the chairman and to thank the ranking member for having this hearing. It is an important hearing. My thanks is going to lead into a line of thought that I would like to have both of you explore. As Mr. DiGregory was answering the question of my colleague from Virginia, we were talking about telephone betting, and so I want to ask you, you have made a point of what Wisconsin's stand is about this.

One of the angsts that I might imagine is amongst those who are in this audience is what seems to be the constant distinction and treatment of this phenomenon called the Internet. We were just the other day looking at cybercrime and there were those, of course, who were aghast because here we go again. There are, of course, those who are looking to tax e-commerce and, of course, have opposition to that.

The telephone has been used for betting. My concern for all of this is the addictive nature, and as I was thinking about using the term addictive, I tried to answer my own question. Well, people can use the telephone. Can you help me, in terms of being a State law enforcement official, what is the unique distinction of the Internet utilization that would require us to act and to intervene in this instance?

Mr. DOYLE. The unique distinction of the Internet is that it is active, immediate, in-time gambling. Unlike telephone gambling, which is mainly laying bets off to bookies over the telephone, what Internet gambling is is essentially putting a gambling machine into everybody's home, so that a 16-year-old sits down at a home computer, and as I indicated, we are not far away from this. As band width increases, as speed of computer increases, the 16-year-old will be sitting at a computer in a home, not laying bets off to a bookie in Chicago from Madison, Wisconsin, but playing a video gambling game right there, just as if that child was in a casino. That is the essential difference of this technology.

Now, let me say, I agree with Mr. DiGregory's call to expand 1084 to make sure that all the prohibitions that apply to the wires also apply to the new kinds of technology, but there are special added concerns that come with the Internet. One of the most interesting things to me is people say, do not look at these technologies differently, and yet we are now hearing for a call for the national Congress to legalize and regulate gambling, despite the policy of many States, because we are now saying they can do it on the Internet.

So this argument cuts both ways. The technology is unique and it does permit direct online gambling, just as if you were sitting in a casino in Las Vegas.

Ms. JACKSON LEE. Mr. DiGregory, I do not want to misstate your position, and as I indicated, I have come in sort of mid-stream, but Mr. Doyle raises an interesting point. Just a few days ago, the Department of Justice was sitting in another hearing talking about cybercrime and we were all trying to figure out how we handle that.

Let me hear from you. This is what I am grappling with. I have some concerns about this legislation, but I know how distinctly technique this tool or this new technology is, and I think the point that Mr. Doyle has raised is the actuality of it being in one's home. I raise an additional point of a more addictive nature than using the telephone. Tell me where you fall in terms of the idea of both of these pieces of legislation, when I say that, answering the uniqueness of it, I think I got from you, or gleaned maybe some reservation, and if you would just highlight that for me, and/or your response if it is not reservation.

Mr. DIGREGORY. My response is that the position that we have taken is that one should not be allowed to engage in Internet gambling from one's home for——

Ms. JACKSON LEE. But take it further in terms of just how far these different pieces of legislation go and if you have any reservations in any one of them.

Mr. CHABOT. Without objection, the gentlelady is granted an additional minute and the witness can respond in that time.

Ms. JACKSON LEE. I thank you, Mr. Chairman. I appreciate your kindness. I saw the red light and I was hoping that he could answer before it went out totally.

Mr. DIGREGORY. Yes, we do have reservations, and one of those reservations is that because the closed-loop subscriber service is defined so broadly, it will essentially allow someone to receive a piece of software, for example, from a business like a youbet.com, which will allow you to, using their software, log onto the Internet and place a bet from your home, wherever you may be, on a horse race which may be occurring in another jurisdiction.

Ms. JACKSON LEE. So you are on the interstate issue, per se, somewhat?

Mr. DIGREGORY. We are on the interstate issue, that is exactly right.

Ms. JACKSON LEE. So you are looking for additional restraints, if you will, to a certain extent, as it impacts interstate commerce or utilization of it through interstate betting?

Mr. DIGREGORY. We do not want to do anything to restrain interstate commerce. All we want to do is make sure that whatever prohibitions are passed are consistent with prohibitions that currently exist. Currently, it is a violation of Section 1084 if you use the telephone to place a bet from your house in State A on a horse race that is taking place in State B, regardless of whether or not State B is sanctioning the race and State B is taking your bet and not somebody in State B who is a bookie. So we think that the bill as drafted, H.R. 3125, will allow something to happen over the Internet that you cannot do today over the telephone.

Ms. JACKSON LEE. It will get through the cracks?

Mr. DIGREGORY. Yes.

Mr. CHABOT. The gentlelady's time has expired.

Ms. JACKSON LEE. I thank you very much, Mr. Chairman. I thank the gentleman very much.

Mr. CHABOT. Thank you. The chair now recognizes the ranking member for an additional minute to ask a final question.

Mr. SCOTT. Thank you. I had two quick questions. Mr. Doyle, are you aware of any prosecutions for gambling on the Internet under present law?

Mr. DOYLE. Yes. Well, in the State of Wisconsin, we have brought three different actions, actually more than that now, but of three different kinds, and we have established in our courts the fact that somebody, even if they have never set foot in the State of Wisconsin, is subject to our gambling laws if they knowingly are taking a bet from somebody in Wisconsin. So we have brought a number of these actions in our State and I know some other State Attorneys General have filed similar kinds of cases.

Mr. SCOTT. Mr. DiGregory, I do not know if you want to answer this now, if you can give us some information. You indicated that you wanted to go after the conduct, not the——

Mr. DIGREGORY. Not the medium.

Mr. SCOTT [continuing]. Medium. I assumed that the wire was in there to give Federal jurisdiction. Do you have a Lopez problem if you go after the conduct and not the medium?

Mr. DIGREGORY. Well, I think you go after the conduct through the medium. What we are saying is simply that you should not have legislation which deals with conduct on one medium differently than the same conduct on a different medium.

Mr. SCOTT. But you would have any interstate medium, is what you are talking about, give you Federal jurisdiction——

Mr. DIGREGORY. Any communication facility, that is right.

Mr. SCOTT. Okay.

Mr. DIGREGORY. And one other point to Ms. Jackson Lee, if I might, I invite you to log on to at least one of these websites, youbet.com, because one of the things that I have seen—it may not still be there, but I have seen in their promotional materials and maybe even on their website is it claims to deliver all the action you get at the track straight to your living room.

Mr. CHABOT. Thank you very much, and we want to thank the panel for their testimony here this afternoon. If they will make their way out, I will introduce the final panel here this afternoon, and if they could come forward as I am introducing them.

The first witness is Mr. Robert Minnix, associate athletic director of Compliance and Legal Affairs at Florida State University. Mr. Minnix also currently serves as chairman of the NCAA Committee on Sportsmanship and Ethical Conduct. He received his undergraduate degree in sociology from Notre Dame University, where he was a star running back. Mr. Minnix also received a juris doctorate from the University of Washington.

From 1975 to 1978, he served as an enforcement representative at the NCAA national office, where he handled matters involving interpretation of rules violations. He also served as Director of Enforcement at the NCAA national office from 1988 to 1995.

Next, we will have testifying Mr. Stephen Walters, chairman of the Oregon Racing Commission and a partner in the law firm of Stowe Rives, LLP. Mr. Walters chairs the Oregon State commission that regulates parimutuel industry horse and dog racing. Oregon's Racing Commission regulates both live horse and dog racing, as well as interstate and intrastate simulcasts of that racing. The five-member Oregon Racing Commission is also responsible for regulating and setting operational policy for all licensed parimutuel industry facilities and participants, which includes policy concerning the use of the new technologies such as the Internet in conjunction with racing activities.

Following his graduation from Stanford University School of Law, Chairman Walters served as a law clerk to U.S. Supreme Court Justice Warren Burger. Since then, he has been engaged in the practice of law in Oregon and California.

The third witness is Mr. Keith S. Whyte, Executive Director of the National Council on Problem Gambling, NCPG. Mr. White oversees the several nationwide programs administered by the NCPG, including a 24-hour confidential help line and a certification program for gambling treatment professionals. Mr. Whyte has also served as Director of Research for the American Gaming Association, where he handled research and public policy issues involving gambling. In addition, Mr. Whyte has published extensively on gambling-related topics and is a frequent speaker at national and international gambling conferences.

Our final witness today is Mr. Bartlett Cleland, Director of the Center for Technology Freedom at the Institute for Policy Innovation. Mr. Cleland's responsibilities include oversight of all technology and related studies, including Internet taxation, technology education and immigration, and intellectual property. He currently serves on the Internet Education Foundation Board of Directors, which involves working closely with the Internet Caucus and such projects as Get Net Wise, a project to assist parents in understanding the Internet and how to protect children online.

Arriving in Washington in 1995, he was Senator John Ashcroft's technology counsel from 1996 until 1998. He is a graduate of Milliken University with a B.S. in philosophy and business administration and received his MBA and law degree from St. Louis University.

In the interest of time, I know that some witnesses have flights around 6 and we do not know what traffic is going to be like. We do not know if we are going to have additional votes, so in the interest of making sure that we are able to conclude this testimony here this afternoon, we ask all the witnesses, please keep to the 5-minute rule. We have got a light there that will go off and tell you. When the red light comes on, time is up, so please try to keep within the 5-minute rule.

We will begin with Mr. Minnix.

STATEMENT OF ROBERT MINNIX, ASSOCIATE ATHLETIC DIRECTOR, FLORIDA STATE UNIVERSITY, TALLAHASSEE, FL

Mr. MINNIX. Mr. Chairman, members of the subcommittee, first of all, thank you for the opportunity to testify on behalf of the National Collegiate Athletic Association in support of H.R. 3125, the Internet Gambling Prohibition Act. The NCAA is a membership organization consisting of nearly 1,000 universities and colleges and it is devoted to the regulation and promotion of intercollegiate athletics for over 330,000 male and female student athletes.

As an athletics administrator at an NCAA member institution, a former NCAA Director of Enforcement, a former student athlete, and the current chair of the NCAA Committee on Sportsmanship and Ethical Conduct, I am acutely aware of the threat that sports gambling poses to the intercollegiate athletics community. Despite Federal and State laws that prohibit sports gambling in nearly every State, this activity remains a growing problem on the campuses and nationwide.

Over the past several years, point shaving scandals on the campuses of Northwestern University and Arizona State University have received widespread media coverage. The impact of these cases must not be minimized. Several of the student athletes involved were indicted and sentenced to serve time in Federal prisons. Coaches and teammates were betrayed and the two schools involved have seen their reputations tarnished. It is clear that sports gambling is not—is not—a victimless crime.

While there is little comprehensive research available that analyzes the prevalence of sports gambling or gambling in general on college campuses, the primary evidence reveals an alarming trend. A 1998 study conducted by the University of Michigan revealed that 35 percent of student athletes gambled on sports while attending college. Over 5 percent of male student athletes wagered on the game in which they participated, provided inside information for gambling purposes, or accepted money for performing poorly in a contest. This result was particularly interesting since NCAA rules strictly prohibit student athletes, coaches, and athletic administrators from engaging in sports gambling activities as they relate to intercollegiate or professional sports events.

Another important research finding reveals that more youth are introduced to gambling through sports betting than through any other type of activity, according to Dr. Howard Shaffer, Director of Harvard University of Medical School's Division on Addiction.

The high incidence of gambling in college campuses, is not just limited to student athletes. It extends to the general student body. A growing consensus of research reveals that the rate of pathological and problem gambling amongst college students are higher than any other segment of the population. As you can see, there is reason to be concerned about the impact of gambling on today's youth. Therefore, it should not be surprising that Internet gambling presents a multitude of new potential dangers for young people.

I work on a college campus and recognize that college students have perhaps the greatest access to the Internet. A student can surf the Web in the library, in a computer lab, or in the privacy of his or her own dormitory room, even in the locker room. Now, with the emergence of Internet gambling, students can wager behind closed doors in virtual privacy. This new phenomenon has raised the fears of those concerned about the threat of sports gambling. Today, the possibility exists for student athletes to place wagers over the Internet and then attempt to influence the outcome of the contest while participating on the court or playing field.

However, the impact of Internet gambling on campus is not a problem that is limited to athletics. If left unchecked, the growth of Internet gambling could be fueled by college students. Offshore Internet gambling operators are aware that students represent a huge potential market. These operators recognize that 70 percent of students have credit cards, and 20 percent of these students have four or more credit cards.

Through its gambling education efforts, the NCAA is hearing from students who, in some cases, gamble their entire tuition or scholarship money away on the Internet. In several of these instances, students have been introduced to Internet sports gambling through advertisements in their student newspapers. Also, aggressive marketing tactics employed by Internet gambling operators have even included in-person solicitation of students at on-campus fraternity houses. Clearly, there is a desperate need for Federal legislation.

For students, the question of whether Internet gambling is legal has caused great confusion. There are advertisements for Internet gambling websites in newspapers, on the radio, and even in inflight magazines.

Mr. CHABOT. Could you wrap up in about a minute, Mr. Minnix?

Mr. MINNIX. Yes, sir. I am just about there. Furthermore, with 650 websites on the web, many students conclude that "if it's on the Internet, it must be legal." Last week, a Wall Street Journal report indicated that two companies are aggressively pursuing online gambling ventures in Nevada in hopes of eventually expanding into other States. The article highlighted the current lack of clarity in U.S. law during a time when experts anticipate an online gambling explosion.

In addition, last month, the Hilton Group announced a series of moves aimed at delivering Internet gambling to wireless platforms. This is part of a $160 million investment. Imagine students wagering on their cell phones. Also, it is clear that the 1961 Wire Act does not cover this type of activity.

I want to conclude by urging this subcommittee to take quick action in adopting Internet gambling prohibition legislation. H.R. 3125 is not a perfect bill, but please do not let the "perfect become the enemy of the good." The House and Senate sponsors have worked several years on trying to craft a bill that has the best chance of passage. If no legislation is adopted, the Internet gambling industry will grow virtually unchecked. The Wire Act has limited viability. It will soon become ineffective as the Internet evolves into a wireless environment. Furthermore, can we realistically expect a 40-year-old law aimed at prohibiting sports gambling over the telephone to be an effective enforcement instrument against this problem?

While considering H.R. 3125, do not overlook its value as a strong deterrent. Experts believe there will soon be a consolidation in the industry that will involve large multi-national corporations entering the field, many with U.S. interests. These companies will have little choice but to recognize and make efforts to comply with any U.S. prohibition against Internet gambling. A Federal prohibition will put an end to any existing legal ambiguities in U.S. law and send a clear message to an industry still in its infancy.

In closing, Internet gambling puts students at risk and strong action from Congress is needed now before we get past the point of no return. Thank you very much.

Mr. CHABOT. Thank you.

[The prepared statement of Mr. Minnix follows:]

PREPARED STATEMENT OF ROBERT MINNIX, ASSOCIATE ATHLETIC DIRECTOR, FLORIDA STATE UNIVERSITY, TALLAHASSEE, FL

Mr. Chairman and members of the Subcommittee, thank you for the opportunity to testify on behalf of the National Collegiate Athletic Association (NCAA) in support of H.R. 3125, the "Internet Gambling Prohibition Act of 1999." The NCAA is a membership organization consisting of nearly 1,000 universities and colleges and is devoted to the regulation and promotion of intercollegiate athletics for over 330,000 male and female student-athletes.

As an athletics administrator at an NCAA member institution, a former NCAA Director of Enforcement and the current chair of the NCAA Committee on Sportsmanship and Ethical Conduct, I am acutely aware of the threat that sports gambling poses to the intercollegiate athletics community. Despite federal and state laws that prohibit sports gambling in nearly every state, this activity remains a growing problem on college campuses and nationwide. Over the past several years, point shaving scandals on the campuses of Northwestern University and Arizona State University have received widespread media coverage. The impact of these cases must not be minimized. Several of the student-athletes involved were indicted and sentenced to serve time in federal prisons. Coaches and teammates were betrayed and the two schools involved have seen their reputations tarnished. It is clear that sports gambling is not a victimless crime.

While there is little comprehensive research available that analyzes the prevalence of sports gambling or gambling in general on college campuses, the preliminary evidence reveals an alarming trend. A 1998 study conducted by the University of Michigan revealed that 35% of student-athletes gambled on sports while attending college. Over 5% of male student-athletes wagered on the game in which they participated, provided inside information for gambling purposes, or accepted money for performing poorly in a contest. This result was particularly interesting since NCAA rules strictly prohibit student-athletes, coaches and athletics administrators from engaging in sports gambling activities as they relate to intercollegiate or professional sporting events. Another important research finding reveals that more youth are introduced to gambling through sports betting than through any other type of activity, according to Dr. Howard Shaffer, director of Harvard University Medical School's Division on Addiction.

The high incidence of gambling on college campuses is not just limited to student-athletes, it extends to the general student body. A growing consensus of research reveals that the rates of pathological and problem gambling among college students are higher than any other segment of the population.

As you can see, there is reason to be concerned about the impact of gambling on today's youth. Therefore, it should not be surprising that Internet gambling presents a multitude of new potential dangers for young people. I work on a college campus and recognize that college students have perhaps the greatest access to the Internet. A student can surf the Web in the library, in a computer lab or in the privacy of his or her own dorm room. Now, with the emergence of Internet gambling, students can wager behind closed doors, in virtual anonymity. This new phenomenon has raised the fears of those concerned about the threat of sports gambling. Today, the possibility exists for student-athletes to place wagers over the Internet and then attempt to influence the outcome of the contest while participating on the court or playing field.

However, the impact of Internet gambling on campus is not a problem that is limited to athletics. If left unchecked, the growth of Internet gambling could be fueled by college students. Offshore Internet gambling operators are aware that students represent a huge potential market. These operators recognize that nearly 70 % of students have credit cards, and 20% have four or more cards. Through its gambling education efforts, the NCAA is hearing from students who, in some cases, gambled their tuition money away on the Internet. In several of these instances, students have been introduced to Internet sports gambling through advertisements in their school newspapers. Also, aggressive marketing tactics employed by Internet gambling operators have even included in-person solicitation of students at on-campus fraternity houses.

Clearly, there is a desperate need for federal legislation. For students, the question of whether Internet gambling is legal has caused great confusion. There are advertisements for Internet gambling Web sites in newspapers, on the radio and even in in-flight magazines. Furthermore, with 650 gambling sites on the Web, many students naively conclude that "if it is on the Internet it must be legal."

Last week, a *Wall Street Journal* report indicated that two companies are aggressively pursuing online sports gambling ventures in Nevada in hopes of eventually expanding into other states. The article highlighted the current lack of clarity in U.S. law during a time when experts anticipate an online gambling explosion. In addition, last month, the Hilton Group announced a series of moves aimed at delivering Internet gambling to wireless platforms. This is part of a $160 million investment. Imagine students wagering on their cell phones? Also, it is clear that the 1961 Wire Act does not cover this type of activity.

I want to conclude by urging this Subcommittee to take quick action in adopting Internet gambling prohibition legislation. H.R. 3125 is not a perfect bill but please do not let "perfect become the enemy of the good." The House and Senate sponsors have worked several years on trying to craft a bill that has the best chance of passage. If no legislation is adopted, the Internet gambling industry will grow virtually unchecked. The Wire Act has limited viability and will soon become ineffective as the Internet evolves into a wireless environment. Furthermore, can we realistically expect a forty year-old law aimed at prohibiting sports gambling over the telephone to be an effective enforcement instrument against this problem?

While considering H. 3125, do not overlook its value as a strong deterrent. Experts believe that there will soon be a consolidation in the industry that will involve large, multi-national corporations entering the field, many with U.S. interests. These companies will have little choice but to recognize and make efforts to comply with any U.S. prohibition against Internet gambling. A federal prohibition will put an end to any existing legal ambiguities in U.S. law and send a clear message to an industry still its infancy. Internet gambling puts students at risk and strong action from Congress is needed now before we get past the point of no return.

Thank you.

Mr. CHABOT. Mr. Walters?

STATEMENT OF STEPHEN WALTERS, CHAIRMAN, OREGON RACING COMMISSION, PORTLAND, OR

Mr. WALTERS. Thank you, Mr. Chairman. I have submitted rather lengthy written testimony and I would commend it to the members of the committee. I do not intend to repeat it all here. I would like to make a few very brief remarks.

As the chairman stated during introductions, I am the chair of the Oregon Racing Commission. I have served on the commission for 9 years. I have been its chair for the past six. The Oregon Racing Commission regulates all aspects of parimutuel wagering and horse and greyhound racing in the State of Oregon. I am here today to testify in support of H.R. 3125 as it was reported out of the subcommittee and particularly to focus my remarks on the provisions of that bill that relate to legal parimutuel wagering in the various States.

As the committee is aware, those provisions include four basic requirements. One, in order to be permissible under this bill, the wagering activity has to be received in a State where it is authorized, licensed, and regulated by the State authorities.

Two, it has to be done over a closed-loop subscriber-based system, which is not the open Internet. It is a system that has various blocking mechanisms to prevent unauthorized use. It must have provisions in the system for identification and age verification.

Three, the wager must originate in a State where parimutuel wagering on that activity, horse or greyhound racing or both, is legal.

And fourth, in the case of horse racing, it must comply with the requirements of the Interstate Horse Racing Act, and it has similar provisions with respect to greyhound racing.

In our view, this bill is appropriate and necessary to preserve the traditional role of State racing commissions, such as the one I chair, in regulating parimutuel wagering on horse and greyhound racing in this country. The Department of Justice is suggesting that no special exceptions should be made for horse and greyhound racing, that it is just like any other type of gambling, and I would respectfully disagree with that and I would cite two fundamental reasons.

The first reason is that horse and greyhound racing is a sporting event. It is conducted in public. The result is easily verifiable. It is presided over by State officials known as stewards who ensure the integrity of the race and it is not one of these, as General Doyle referred to, games where you do not know what the other person's hand is. It is a public sporting event. It has been legal for a long time in this country. The overwhelming majority of States have legalized wagering on horse racing. I believe it is 43 out of 50.

In the State of Oregon, not only is it a public sporting event, but it is very important economically to our State. It provides 5,000 jobs. In Oregon, that is a lot. They are not simply jobs, people taking bets and processing wagers. They are jobs in the agricultural industry. Those jobs would not exist if the Department of Justice's view of this bill and of various statutes were to be adopted, and I will elaborate on that a little more in just one moment.

The second distinction between horse and greyhound racing is that it has a long history of comprehensive and successful State regulation in this country. Account wagering has been legal in a number of States from 30 to 20 years. That is placing wagers using the telephone, and that wagering has taken place over State lines, subject to the authority and the regulation of the State commissions in the State where it is received.

Commingling of pools, which again is transmission of wagering, wagers from one State to another State on a race based in that State, has been practiced in this country legally and regulated thoroughly for at least the past decade, if not longer. This has been a successful program of regulation and we respectfully submit that the committee should allow that to proceed in this bill.

I would like to just close with some brief remarks about the type of regulation we have in Oregon, and I want to focus on one aspect in particular. We have had a lot of testimony on problems of addictive gambling, on responsible wagering, and that is something that is very important to our Racing Commission. We insist that in connection with maintaining account wagering in the State of Oregon in licensing interstate simulcasting hubs, that the licensees develop and maintain programs for responsible wagering. This includes cooling off periods when you replenish your account. You cannot simply log onto the Internet, fire up your account, and spend all night playing at the racetrack. Similarly, we require that they develop other resources and other programs for ensuring responsible wagering.

There are a number of other respects in which our rules are comprehensive and go beyond the requirements of this bill and we respectfully request that the committee pass out the bill in this form and that the House adopt it so that we can maintain our historical role in regulating this important industry. Thank you very much.

Mr. CHABOT. Thank you.

[The prepared statement of Mr. Walters follows:]

PREPARED STATEMENT OF STEPHEN WALTERS, CHAIRMAN, OREGON RACING COMMISSION, PORTLAND, OR

I appreciate this opportunity to present the views of the horse industry on H.R. 3125, the "Internet Gambling Prohibition Act."

I am testifying today in my capacity as Chairman of the Oregon State Racing Commission, which regulates all matters pertaining to the conduct of horseracing and dog racing and pari-mutuel wagering on such activities that occur within the State of Oregon.

THE PARI-MUTUEL RACING AND BREEDING INDUSTRY

Pari-mutuel horse racing, including off-track and inter-track wagering is legal in 43 states and involves the racing of Thoroughbreds, Standardbreds, Quarter Horses, Arabians, Appaloosas and Paints. There are over 175 racetracks in the U.S. Racing and racehorse breeding is a widespread and diverse industry that includes gambling, sport, recreation and entertainment and is built upon an agricultural base that involves the breeding and training of the horses.

Economic Impact

According to the study of the Economic Impact of the Horse Industry in the United States done by Barents Group, LLC, the economic and fiscal consulting unit of KPMG Peat Marwick LLP, for the American Horse Council Foundation, racing and racehorse breeding have a total economic impact in the U.S. of $34 billion and generate 472,800 total full-time-equivalent jobs. There are 941,000 people and 725,000 horses involved in the racing industry.

Wagering on horse racing is permitted in 43 states and there is an active horse breeding and training business in all 50 states. In many, the economic contribution of the racing and breeding industry to state and local economies is substantial and the industry ranks among the state's most significant economic entities. For example, in Florida, it involves 37,000 horses, has a $2.1 billion economic impact and generates 27,300 full-time equivalent jobs; in California it involves 69,000 horses, has a $4.1 billion economic impact and generates 52,000 FTE jobs; in Illinois, it involves 52,000 horses, has a $2 billion economic impact and generates 30,700 FTE jobs; in Ohio, it involves 40,000 horses, has a $1.3 billion economic impact and generates 17,000 FTE jobs; and in Texas, it involves 74,000 horses, has a $1.8 billion economic impact and generates 27,900 jobs.

Pari-mutuel racing generates over $500 million annually in direct state and local revenue from pari-mutuel taxes, track licenses, occupational licenses, admission taxes and miscellaneous fees.

Racing as a Sport

Racing is an activity that attracts many fans who appreciate it and follow it as a sport and who enjoy the excitement of the race and the athletic ability of the horses. The Triple Crown races are considered among the most important sporting events conducted in the United States each year and are widely reported in the sports media. Over 130 additional hours of top Thoroughbred races are broadcast on national television each year, including the Breeders' Cup and the NTRA Champions on Fox Series. The national championships of Standardbred and Quarter Horse racing are also televised nationally and widely covered by the media. In addition, most major U.S. newspapers cover racing and print the results of the races at their local tracks on a daily basis, much like they print the box scores of other sports.

The Pari-Mutuel System

While horseracing is a sport on which one can gamble, it would be erroneous to assume that pari-mutuel wagering is the same as other forms of gambling. Unlike most other forms of gambling, horseracing uses the pari-mutuel system in which bettors wager against one another instead of against the "house." Of the total amount wagered on a particular race, approximately 80% is returned to winning bettors. The other 20%, called the "takeout," is shared between the state government, the racetrack and the horsemen who race at the track. Takeout rates, which vary from state to state, are published in track programs, which are available at race tracks and at simulcast wagering sites away from the track, so that fans know the rates and how they might affect their wagering.

Wagering computations are accomplished by a totalisator machine, a computer, which adds bets over and over again during the course of betting. Every 30 to 60 seconds the "tote" flashes new betting totals and odds for each horse. The machines contain a number of features designed to minimize the potential for pari-mutuel fraud or machine malfunction. These features include coded ticket paper and duplication of all critical functions by two computers working independently of one another.

I point this out because the pari-mutuel system and the published information available ensures that the public has easy access to data regarding their true chances of winning. There is little chance of manipulating the odds and therefore the payouts. The use of the tote machine allows bettors to determine their chances of winning every 30 to 60 seconds. In addition, the race upon which the wager is made, and paid, is a public event, watched by fans at the track or off-track facility, often viewed by others on television or cable, and always overseen by the stewards at the track itself and the state racing commission to ensure the integrity of the race.

In 1998, over 30 million people attended the races and wagered over $14 billion, approximately 80% of which was returned to the winning players.

FEDERAL AND STATE POLICIES ON GAMBLING

Gambling, including that conducted on horseracing, has always been of concern to the federal and state governments. Throughout American history, the prohibition or legalization and regulation of gambling has primarily been a function of the states. The only time that the federal government has become involved has been when one or more states could not solve a problem without federal intervention. But even in these instances, for the reasons discussed above and others, pari-mutuel racing has often been either treated differently or specifically considered under federal gambling laws. The racing industry has developed to its current status under a regulatory framework of state law and regulation and the Interstate Horseracing Act of 1978 (discussed below). If racing and breeding hopes to continue to compete in today's economy, it must be able to continue to do so under these same statutes.

State Regulation—A Long History

Pari-mutuel racing has been conducted in the United States under state authority and regulation for over 75 years. In every state that has allowed legalized wagering on horseracing, strict state oversight and regulation has accompanied its introduction and growth. In each state the pari-mutuel industry is regulated by an agency most commonly known as the state racing commission. Among commission prerogatives are the licensing of track and horse owners, trainers, jockeys, drivers and all others involved in the pari-mutuel sport, and the promulgation and enforcement of the specific regulations under which the industry must operate. All matters pertaining to the operation of pari-mutuel racing, including wagering, are regulated by these agencies on behalf of the governors and state legislatures.

Over the years the states have consistently acted on the perceived need to closely regulate legal wagering and protect the public's interest in pari-mutuel sports. The actions of state legislatures and the racing commissions which carry out their policies have been predicated on the desire to: (1) maintain the integrity of the events on which the public is allowed to wager; (2) oversee the state's tax-related and economic interest in that wagering; (3) ensure that licensees meet specific standards of qualification; and (4) control any unsavory elements which may attempt to associate with the wagering aspects of the sport.

The Interstate Horseracing Act of 1978

In 1978, Congress enacted a federal statute that specifically deals with interstate gambling on horseracing. The Interstate Horseracing Act of 1978 ("IHA") made clear that a racetrack controlled wagering on its races in interstate and international commerce and provided for industry and regulatory approvals before betting was permitted between jurisdictions where the wagering was legal.

In the findings to the IHA, Congress said that states have the primary responsibility for determining what forms of gambling may take place within their borders, but that the Federal government should prevent interference by one state with the gambling policies of another. In the IHA Congress provided that with respect to the limited area of interstate off-track wagering on horse racing:

> There is a need for Federal action to ensure that States will continue to cooperate with one another in the acceptance of legal interstate wagers.

Importantly, in passing the IHA, Congress specifically recognized that "pari-mutuel horseracing is a significant industry which provides substantial revenue to the States" and that "properly regulated and properly conducted interstate off-track betting may contribute substantial benefits to the States and the horseracing industry."

Consistent with these findings, Congress stated as a matter of congressional findings and policy that:

> It is the policy of Congress in this chapter to regulate interstate commerce with respect to wagering on horseracing, in order to further the horse racing and legal off-track betting industries in the United States.

The combination of state statutes and regulations and the IHA have provided the racing industry with a workable regulatory framework for over two decades that has allowed the industry to develop its current activities within clear parameters and guidelines.

CURRENT ACTIVITIES OF RACING

The dissemination of information about racing, simulcasting, off-track and intertrack wagering, common pool wagering and account wagering have been initiated, operated and expanded under the IHA and state approval, licensing and regulation.

Information

Communication today is very complicated in the highly complex and ever-changing technological world. In this environment new industries have sprung up virtually overnight forcing existing industries to adapt and change practices in order to compete for the public's support. This is particularly true in the areas of wagering and entertainment.

Like others, the horseracing industry has had to adapt and change dramatically in the face of exploding competition and new technology. An example of that is that many racetracks, horsemen's associations and private businesses are now advertising and offering information on the sport through various media, both traditional and more technological state-of-the-art, including the Internet.

The process of betting on horse racing and selecting the winner is called "handicapping." It is a cerebral process for serious bettors who spend a great deal of time at the track, and elsewhere, pouring over information that will help them select the winners of races. For students of the sport this is not a random selection. The "handicapping" information used in this process has been available in written forms since racing began and is similar to the statistical information available for other sports.

The racing industry is presently offering a great deal of this type of "handicapping" information in publications, on-the-wire, over toll-free numbers and over the Internet in the form of advertisements for state-licensed and regulated race tracks, information and "how-to" sites, "tout" sheets, past performance information, betting lines and similar information, that will market the racing product to new fans and allows existing patrons to participate more successfully.

This continued flow of this information is critical to the racing business and we submit should not be affected by any changes to current law.

Simulcasting and Common Pool Wagering

Prior to 1970, legal pari-mutuel wagering on racing was limited to those at the track where the race was run. In 1970, the New York legislature approved off-track wagering. As an aside, at that time the computerized system operated by New York OTB (Off-Track-Betting) was one of the first real-time, on-line computer systems in the U.S. Since then, many states, and the federal government under the Interstate Horseracing Act, have authorized racetracks to simulcast or transmit signals of their races off-track into other states and jurisdictions under applicable law.

With the continued development of technology, by the early 1980s racing was able to make its product better for its patrons again. Additional technological changes allowed the linking of pari-mutuel wagering pools among tracks in separate jurisdictions, called "commingled pools," so that payouts could better reflect the size and wagering behavior of the entire betting public.

The racing industry's continuing utilization of state-of-the-art technology has resulted in the ability of the industry to survive and offer its patrons a better product. In fact, today over eighty percent of the money wagered on racing is bet at facilities or locations other than where the race itself is run. Again, all with the approval and regulation of the states involved.

Account Wagering

Another process for pari-mutuel wagering on racing that has expanded over the two last decades is account wagering, primarily telephone betting. Currently, eight States, including Connecticut, Kentucky, Maryland, Nevada, Ohio, Oregon, Pennsylvania and New York, have enacted legislation specifically authorizing the acceptance of account wagers by licensed facilities within those States and a number of others are considering similar legislation. For example, California is currently considering legislation that would allocate the proceeds from account wagering by California residents among the California pari-mutuel industry.

Account wagering is not a new activity in the United States. Telephone account betting has been offered in New York for over 25 years by New York City Off Track Betting and upstate New York Off Track Betting entities—all state agencies. These entities have accepted wagers from residents of New York and other states who had established accounts in New York.

In order to keep pace with modern technological advances, the horseracing industry needs to be able to continue these activities, provided that such activities are conducted in accordance the IHA and applicable state laws or regulations.

In summary, the IHA and individual state statutes and regulations, under the supervision of state racing commissions, combine to form a very capable regulatory system for pari-mutuel racing.

THE INTERNET GAMBLING PROHIBITION ACT OF 1999—H.R. 3125

The Internet Gambling Prohibition Act of 1999, H.R. 3125, is a natural response to the current changes in technology. The regulated and licensed pari-mutuel horse racing industry agrees with the intent of this legislation, as characterized by Congressman Bob Goodlatte when he introduced a previous version of H.R. 3125 in 1997:

> . . . this legislation does not preempt any state laws, does not cover online news reporting about gambling, and does not apply to transactions that are legal in both the State in which they originate and the state in which they are received.

The regulation of gambling is essential to protect state policies and revenues, the racing industry's ability to control its own product and the integrity of racing. Our industry is opposed to any unregulated or unauthorized gambling, particularly on racing.

Nonetheless, this legislation involves very complicated legal and technical issues. We believe the exemptions in the current legislation that allow horseracing to continue to conduct its existing activities are fair and consistent with existing law and practice under which horseracing has operated for decades. We are concerned, however, about any changes to the current legislation that may adversely impact what racing is doing now under state regulation and the IHA with respect to the dissemination of information, common pooling and account wagering.

The worst possible result for all concerned would be to enact legislation that would restrict licensed and regulated entities from conducting their current business using modern technology with the result being that many of those who wish to wager on horseracing will be forced to deal with unlicensed and unregulated vendors, either off-shore or operating illegally within the United States. This would open the door to consumer fraud and result in significant decreases in revenues for the licensed operators, purses (which are directly derived from licensed wagering revenues) and tax revenues for the Federal and State governments.

It is critical to the future of the racing industry, the agri-business it supports, the state revenue and employment it generates, the sporting and the entertainment benefits it provides to countless fans, that all distribution mechanisms of racing information and its product be available, so long as they continue to meet regulatory criteria established by state governments and comply with the IHA. It is also critical that the racing industry have the opportunity to take advantage of any and all technological advancements in the future distribution of its information and products in order to successfully compete against other forms of gambling, sport and entertainment.

Because of the unique status of pari-mutuel racing and the present regulatory structure applicable to it, we believe that the purposes of this legislation and the particular needs of racing can both be accommodated without infringing on federal or state public policies, abrogating strict regulation or lessening the current protections of the public. We look forward to working with the Chairman of the Subcommittee, the sponsors of the bill, the members of the committee and the staff to accomplish this.

Justice Department Comments

In the context of the above remarks, we would also like to address the comments submitted by the Justice Department to the Senate Judiciary Committee last summer during its consideration of the Senate version of the Interstate Gambling Prohibition Act and similar comments recently submitted to the New York State Racing and Wagering Board.

These comments can be summarized as questioning the legality under the Wire Act (18 U.S.C. 1084) of the current practices of interstate simulcasting, commingling of pools and account wagering and opposing exemptions to the Internet Gambling Prohibition Act that would allow racing to continue to conduct these activities using modern technology. We believe this is an extreme and incorrect interpretation of the Wire Act that disregards the specific purpose behind the Wire Act of combating organized crime, the passage by Congress of the Interstate Horseracing Act of 1978, and the reality that State sanctioned and licensed businesses have been conducting these activities in compliance with existing State and federal laws for over twenty years.

The Wire Act is undeniably directed at illegal gambling and bookmaking conducted by organized crime. It was enacted 1961 as part of a package of bills directed against organized crime and racketeering. *See The Attorney General's Program to Curb Organized Crime and Racketeering*, Hearings before Committee on the Judiciary, U.S. Senate, 87th Cong., 1st Sess. (1961).

In its report accompanying the Wire Act, the House Committee on the Judiciary wrote that:

> "The purpose of the bill is to assist the various States and the District of Columbia in the enforcement of their laws pertaining to gambling, bookmaking and like offenses and to aid in the suppression of organized gambling activities. . . ."

Any fair reading of the Wire Act and the Congressional record accompanying the Act makes clear that the Wire Act is not directed at nor intended to make illegal licensed state regulated activities.

The Wire Act was enacted in 1961. Seventeen years later, Congress enacted the Interstate Horseracing Act of 1978 for the express purposes of ensuring proper regulation of "interstate off-track betting" and "furthering the horseracing and legal off-track betting industries in the United States." The interpretation of the Wire Act currently propounded by the Justice Department would appear to disregard Congress' enactment of the IHA and the supporting Congressional record.

Lastly, although the Wire Act was enacted almost 40 years ago and interstate simulcasting and account wagering have been conducted in this country since the early 1970s, neither the Justice Department nor any federal prosecutors have ever used the Wire Act to prosecute any state licensed and regulated entities for conducting interstate simulcasting, commingling of pools or account wagering. The reasons for this should be clear. The legislative history of the Wire Act, coupled with the passage of the IHA and the existing framework of extensive state regulation leads to the inescapable conclusion that the Wire Act simply does not apply to the licensed regulated sport of horseracing.

Stated another way, the logical conclusion of the Justice Department's current position would render criminally illegal interstate wagering on legal, state-regulated horseracing that currently provides hundreds of millions of dollars in annual tax revenues, supports hundreds of thousands of jobs, and has been an ongoing state-sanctioned activity for decades.

In conclusion, the current form of H.R. 3125 has been carefully crafted to allow the sport of horseracing to continue to conduct its business in the same way it has been operating for the last two decades. The bill does not in any way expand wagering, but instead preserves the status quo. We appreciate the opportunity to present these comments on this important legislation and would be happy to respond to any questions.

Mr. CHABOT. Mr. Whyte?

STATEMENT OF KEITH S. WHYTE, EXECUTIVE DIRECTOR, NATIONAL COUNCIL ON PROBLEM GAMBLING, WASHINGTON, DC

Mr. WHYTE. Mr. Chairman, members of the committee, thank you very much for the opportunity to testify on this bill on behalf of the National Council on Problem Gambling, the Nation's oldest and largest organization dedicated to addressing issues of problem gambling.

Since 1972, we have worked with the Federal, State, tribal, and local governments, the gaming industry, and other nonprofit organizations on gambling issues. We have consistently maintained a position of neutrality, neither supporting nor opposing gaming. The mission of the National Council is to increase public awareness of pathological gambling, to insure the availability of treatment for problem gamblers and their families, and to encourage research and programs for prevention and education.

The National Council neither supports nor opposes H.R. 3125. We are concerned about the impact of Internet gambling on individuals who may have gambling problems and we are also concerned about the exemptions contained within the bill. We applaud the bill's sponsors and their supporters for their concern about Internet gambling and certainly support their call for increased Federal attention in this area, a recommendation that was echoed by the National Gambling Impact Study Commission.

We also recognize that, historically, Federal efforts to address gambling have been riddled with exemptions and the regulation and enforcement have traditionally been conducted on the State level. We are not taking a position on existing Internet-related activity conducted under current Federal or State law.

While we remain neutral on the legality and even the desirability of Internet wagering, we recognize that Internet gambling may create additional risk factors for problem gambling, including social isolation and unlimited access to the wagering. Online gambling, as with any other form of legal or illegal gambling, may be abused by individuals with gambling problems. Furthermore, the availability of Internet gambling may act as a trigger for relapse of pathological gamblers who have struggled into recovery. Our primary concern is for the approximately one to 2 percent of the U.S. adult population that is currently estimated to be suffering from a pathological gambling disorder.

Several witnesses today have raised the issue of minors gambling. We would note that, historically in the United States, minors have double the prevalence rates of gambling problems and that has been a consistent statistic for the last 20 years. We urge greater Federal and State attention to the education, prevention, public awareness, research, and treatment of this disorder.

Although H.R. 3125 prohibits many types of Internet wagering, it also contains exemptions that allow several sectors of the U.S. gaming industry to conduct Internet gambling. Between the State lotteries and the parimutuel industry, more than half the U.S. legal gaming industry by revenue would be allowed to offer some type of interactive Internet wagering. Therefore, this bill is a selected expansion as well as a limited prohibition of Internet gambling.

We are particularly concerned that specific language in the bill may open the door to minors betting on the Internet. The patchwork of different rules and regulations for gambling in each State result in different legal ages for each type of activity in many States. I would note that in Illinois, you can gamble on the lottery at 18, blackjack and craps, you have to be 21, unless it is run by a charity, and then you can be 18. But the minimum age for horse racing in Illinois is 17.

Section (A)(2)(c) of the bill prohibits minors from gambling over a closed-loop subscriber-based system, but Section (A)(2)(b) allows persons to gamble from home if it is operated in accordance with the rules of the State. We are concerned that this provision could be interpreted as permitting minors who are allowed to gamble under Illinois law to participate in at-home gambling on parimutuel events, as sanctioned under this bill. Gambling is an adult activity and is never appropriate for minors.

The NCPG also recommends the inclusion of additional responsible gaming provisions in this bill. Sections (A)(2)(b) and (A)(2)(c) set conditions under which this interactive wagering is possible, including the restriction on minors and the requirement of an age verification system. We would support the inclusion of additional language, including many of the things that Mr. Walters has talked about. The addition of these minimum standards may encourage an individual with a gambling problem to seek the appropriate help, and we would certainly be happy to work with the committee and other representatives on these. Again, the bill sets the precedent for some restrictions or limitations and we would like to carry that further.

We believe that any discussion of gambling should include information on the potential health risk of problem and pathological gambling. It is also our belief that there is a need for increased public awareness and prevention efforts anywhere that gambling, legal or illegal, is available.

In conclusion, I would like to thank the committee for an opportunity to present our views on this bill and would be happy to answer any questions.

Mr. CHABOT. Thank you very much.

[The prepared statement of Mr. Whyte follows:]

PREPARED STATEMENT OF KEITH S. WHYTE, EXECUTIVE DIRECTOR, NATIONAL COUNCIL ON PROBLEM GAMBLING, WASHINGTON, DC

Chairman Hyde and the members of the Committee on the Judiciary, Subcommittee on Crime, thank you for the opportunity to testify before this committee on behalf of the National Council on Problem Gambling, the nation's oldest and largest organization dedicated to addressing problem gambling. Since 1972 the National Council on Problem Gambling (NCPG) has worked with Federal, state, tribal and local governments, industry and other non-profit groups on problem gambling issues. We have consistently maintained a position of neutrality, neither supporting nor opposing gaming.

The mission of the National Council on Problem Gambling is to increase public awareness of pathological gambling, ensure the widespread availability of treatment for problem gamblers and their families, and to encourage research and programs for prevention and education.

The National Council administers several nationwide programs, including a 24-hour confidential helpline, a gambling-specific certification program for treatment professionals, and sponsors the *Journal of Gambling Studies*, the only academic journal in the world devoted to problem gambling research. In addition, the NCPG sponsors regional, national and international conferences, supports research, distributes literature and works with other organizations involved in problem gambling issues. The National Council on Problem Gambling is a tax-exempt, non-profit corporation.

The NCPG currently has 34 state affiliate chapters, and corporate and individual members. They encompass the leading United States and international experts in problem gambling policy, research, prevention, education and treatment. We represent individuals, families and loved ones affected by problem and pathological gambling.

The NCPG neither supports or opposes HR 3125, the Internet Gambling Prohibition Act of 1999. We are concerned about the impact of internet gambling on individuals who may have gambling problems and we are concerned about the exemptions for new operations in this bill.

We applaud the bill sponsors and supporters for their concern about internet gambling, and certainly support their call for increased Federal attention in this area, as recommended by the National Gambling Impact Study Commission (NGISC).

We also recognize that historically, Federal efforts to address gambling have been riddled with exemptions, and that regulation and enforcement have been conducted at the state level. Furthermore, we are not taking a position on existing gambling-related activity conducted under current state or Federal law.

While the NCPG remains neutral on the legality or desirability of online wagering, we recognize that internet gambling may create additional risk factors, including social isolation and unlimited access. What we do know, however, is that online gambling, as with any other form of legal or illegal gambling, may be abused by individuals with gambling problems. Furthermore, the availability of internet gambling may act as a trigger for relapse for pathological gamblers in recovery. Our primary concern is for the approximately 1–2% of the U.S. adult population estimated to be currently suffering from the serious mental health disorder of pathological gambling. We urge greater Federal and state attention to the education, public awareness, prevention, treatment and research of this disorder.

Although HR 3125 prohibits many types of internet wagering, it also contains exemptions that allow several sectors of the U.S gaming industry to conduct internet gambling. Of these groups, state lotteries alone accounted for approximately $25 billion in gaming revenue last year, almost half of the total U.S. gaming revenue. When parimutuel wagering industry is added in, more than half the U.S. legal gaming industry by revenue would be allowed to offer at-home wagering. Nearly four-fifths of the states have lotteries, parimutuel facilities or both. Therefore, this bill is a selective expansion as well as a limited prohibition of internet gambling.

We are particularly concerned that current language in this bill may open the door to minors betting on the Internet. As you know, each state determines the legality and regulation of each form of gaming. Unfortunately, as the NGISC noted, few states have approached this with a consistent public policy. The result is a patchwork of differing rules and regulations for each type of gaming in a state. Most notably, this results in differing legal ages for different forms of gaming. Illinois is one such state. While the minimum legal age to play the lottery is 18 years old, blackjack and craps players in a riverboat casino must be 21 years old, unless the blackjack and craps are operated by a charity, where individuals 18 and older can gamble. Minors are allowed to bet on parimutuel racing at the age of 17 in the state of Illinois.

Section (a)(2)(C) of the bill prohibits "access by any person . . . who is a minor" but Section (a)(2)(B) allows persons to gamble from home if the system is operated ". . . in accordance with the laws of the State in which it is located. . . ." We are concerned that this provision could be interpreted as permitting minors, who are allowed to gamble under Illinois law, to participate in the at-home gambling sanctioned under this bill. Gambling is an adult activity and is never appropriate for minors.

The NCPG also recommends the inclusion of additional responsible gaming provisions into the bill. Sections (a)(2)(B) and (C) set conditions under which interactive wagering is permissible, including the restriction on minors and the requirement of a positive age-verification system. We suggest the inclusion of additional language to reduce the impact on problem gamblers. In particular, we support placing limits on the amount wagered per transaction and per session or day. We support requiring at least a 12-hour waiting period between the deposit of gaming funds and their availability. We support requiring operators to post problem-gambling helplines and responsible gaming messages encouraging customers to seek help if they have a problem. The addition of these minimum standards may encourage an individual with a gambling problem to seek appropriate help. We would be happy to work with staff and industry representatives on these and additional measures to help mitigate problem gambling. These suggested additions follow the precedent set by the customer and age verification system and data standards requirements in the existing legislation.

We believe that any discussion of gambling should include information on the potential health risk of problem and pathological gambling. It is also our belief that there is a need for increased public awareness and prevention efforts anywhere that gambling, legal or illegal, is available.

In conclusion, I would like to thank the committee for the opportunity to present our views on this issue. I would be happy to respond to any questions.

Mr. CHABOT. Mr. Cleland?

STATEMENT OF BARTLETT D. CLELAND, ESQ., POLICY DIRECTOR, CENTER FOR TECHNOLOGY FREEDOM, LEWISVILLE, TX

Mr. CLELAND. Good afternoon, Mr. Chairman, members of the committee. The Center for Technology Freedom was created to explain to the American people and policy makers the policy changes posed by technological changes and the economy and to point a way for the society that will encourage free markets, free minds, and a free people. In this instance, I think there are four important issues, among some of the others I denote in my written testimony. The top four are consistency, Internet operations, States' rights, and enforcement.

For every citizen, the legislation should be very troubling. The bill broadens the scope of government sanctioned gaming. Closed-loop subscriber services, as we have heard described, gambling for horse and dog races would be given a nod of approval by the Federal Government for the potential of in-home gambling. Lotteries and hotel casinos are also excepted from the act and thereby seemingly are given some sort of legitimacy, not by our States but by our Nation's Government.

Given the realities of the Internet and the language of this legislation, what you end up with is a law that liberalizes gambling. The floor statements touting the need for a Federal Government ban on Internet gaming emphasizes the importance of protecting our country from rampant gambling. I can understand those sentiments. What I cannot understand is how this legislation even begins to measure up. The multiple carve-outs for special interests make a mockery of the legislation in the first place and make the prospect for prohibiting Internet gambling more impossible than an absolute ban.

I am baffled at how the Federal Government on one hand says that gambling is eroding our values, placing our children at risk, and fostering addiction, but then in the same legislation it says that if certain gambling occurs or in a particular way, then we are okay. Either gaming is okay and we merely want to protect the analog world or gambling is indeed harmful and we should actually prohibit gambling. Well, maybe the message is the devil is okay in small amounts and so long as he does not hop on his laptop.

Greatly problematic from an operations standpoint is the prohibition on content. Putting aside all the legal issues at hand, how do you really expect this to work? How do you propose to stop a foreign-operated site that advertises gambling and maybe even offers online gambling? What happens if the advertising is on a radio station in Europe or in the Caribbean that we listen to via the Internet? Are the travel websites that offer vacation packages to jurisdictions where gaming is legal now going to be legal in a jurisdiction where gaming is illegal?

Interesting, I hear advertisements for casinos all the time in Dallas, where gambling is not legal, for casinos in Louisiana, where gambling is allowed. Why would we treat the Internet any differently? In fact, we should not treat the Internet differently, although I understand the great temptation to do so.

The simple answer is that you cannot selectively winnow content from the Internet with Federal legislation. Now, some elected officials have recently said they would vow to pull the plug on lines that "bring in objectionable content." You have me there. Federal legislation could at that point stop objectionable content. We could set about creating a tele-Internet communications isolationist country, a gigantic closed-loop subscriber-based system.

For that matter, this entire approach assumes that some purveyor is sending material into the U.S. or into any particular State or arbitrary political subdivision. That notion is entirely wrong. The Internet as a creation and its original design was developed to survive a nuclear war. You need to consider that fact very carefully as you try to partition off sections of the Internet.

How is legislation going to accomplish it? That question has never been answered because there is no solution that allows the Internet to continue to operate as it does and quash specific content.

How about a real world example. No government in the world allows child pornography. However, it still exists, even with making the supply and demand a criminal action. Okay, now take other pornography, let us say in a jurisdiction that outlaws supplies. Do you believe that right now that it cannot be viewed on the Internet in those places? Remember that individuals go online 11 times more often to view pornography than they do to gamble, a much bigger issue to resolve and we still cannot conceive of an effective solution.

This legislation will be just as porous, no restriction on demand and many foreign governments looking to protect their growth industries. If we really are opposed to Internet gambling, why not make demand a criminal conduct, as well? In fact, if we just stop for a moment and consider how things really work, the system is not hard to understand. We will use your Congressional websites as an example.

Now, I am sure that many of you have sites available to your constituents. Those sites do not go out to people. Individuals visit your sites. To be absolutely precise, individuals direct their computer to search out a particular website. They direct their computer to the server in your office which holds the information for which they are searching. Then they view the information on their computer that has collected the information sent back to them in data packets. The bottom line is that information would not have gotten to their computer but for their request. To say otherwise is to say that you actually desire those telecommuting calls during your evening dinner.

By permitting some types of gambling despite the prohibition, the bill is a Federal endorsement of gambling expansion. At the same time, enforcement is absolutely impossible, given the technological realities of the Internet. For gambling opponents, one simply has to balance the greater evil, gambling or the end of the Internet.

Finally, despite the claims that this legislation does not impact State rights, it absolutely does. The public comment points out a list of items that are not preempted at the State level but utterly ignores the fact that if a State found it appropriate to allow gambling on the Internet, it would not be allowed to do so. We are well aware that Internet gambling will continue. Right now, nearly 50 countries allow and regulate such gambling. Again, even the most basic understanding of the Internet, we can appreciate that websites will be available for viewing and interaction in the United States. This is not just a hypothetical issue. The State of Minnesota is creating a commission to look at the benefits of licensing Internet gaming operations.

One of the true and as yet unrealized promises of the Internet is that geography becomes irrelevant. Unfortunately, Congress has continued in trying to end that promise. Passing legislation before a critical analysis of such issues such as nexus could be disastrous not just in this legislation, but in legislation related to all the Internet.

Mr. CHABOT. We are over the 5 minutes, so if you could wrap up within a minute, that would be great.

Mr. CLELAND. I will do so. Thank you.

Mr. CHABOT. Thank you.

Mr. CLELAND. In fact, the legislation is full of implications for nexus. A casual review demonstrates that in regards to Indian lands the term "on" is used, clearly a nexus issue. In addition, the very definitions are rife with decisions regarding nexus, such as a person buying a lottery ticket must be physically located in the State for the lottery for which he or she will partake.

We should consider the words such as "receiving," as in receiving a bet or wager. Where is the bet or wager received, at the server or at a personal computer? Should it matter? We are living in a world that no longer needs to cling to a definition of place as defined by geography. A conscious decision may be made to govern Federal affairs by geography, but understand that this should be a conscious decision made with the understanding of the broad implications for the Internet and technology.

Ironically, a decision on the nexus issue here easily leads to a decision regarding Internet taxation, a result I am sure that many in this body would like to avoid.

With so many countries allowing gaming, it is a safe bet that this legislation will not be able to effectively prohibit Americans from placing a bet on, say, the St. Louis Rams via e-mail. Why should this matter? I cannot find anywhere in the legislation any attempt to deal with operators who are beyond the reach of U.S. law enforcement.

In summary, then, Internet gambling is the canary in the coal mine. If the legislation that you have before you passes, we will know that the prospect of a regulation-free Internet was simply far too great of a threat to those who feel the need to exercise unrestrained Federal Government control. Passage will demonstrate that, regardless of topic, special interests will be able to exempt themselves in the chaos of legislative drafting. If this is truly the case, too bad for the Internet, too bad for our rule of law, and too bad for those who are opposed to gaming as a matter of principle.

Mr. CHABOT. Thank you very much.

[The prepared statement of Mr. Cleland follows:]

PREPARED STATEMENT OF BARTLETT D. CLELAND, ESQ., POLICY DIRECTOR, CENTER FOR TECHNOLOGY FREEDOM, LEWISVILLE, TX

INTRODUCTION

Good afternoon Mr. Chairman, and members of the sub-committee. I am Bartlett Cleland, the Director of the Center for Technology Freedom (CTF), of the Institute for Policy Innovation (IPI). The Institute for Policy Innovation is a free-market "think tank" dedicated to promoting lower taxes, fewer regulations, and a smaller, less-intrusive federal government. IPI currently focuses on tax cuts, long-term tax reform, educational choice, high-tech and Internet issues, and the rollback of harmful and counterproductive regulations. IPI is a public foundation, supported wholly by contributions from individuals, businesses, and other non-profit foundations. IPI neither solicits nor accepts funds from any government agency, and is recognized by the IRS as a 501(c)(3) charitable organization.

The views expressed in my testimony are my opinions and do not necessarily reflect the views of the Institute for Policy Innovation or the Center for Technology Reform or its directors.

You know, I thought that I did all I could in my career to avoid being called to testify by the minority members of this committee. I began my political activism at 15 in the Reagan Roundup, then, later, worked for Senator John Ashcroft as his technology counsel. I handled all technology issues and most prominently intellectual property, encryption, Internet tax, and regulatory issues of the Internet. I then went to work for Grover Norquist and Americans for Tax Reform for a year and a half as his technology and policy counsel. I had some real grassroots experience and had the opportunity to fight on the taxpayer's behalf. Now I am directing the free-market Center for Technology Freedom.

The Center for Technology Freedom believes that the rapid proliferation of technology in all areas of life including communications, health, education, commerce and entertainment has spawned a new and different economy. This technologically driven economy is not limited to computers and the Internet, but in fact encompasses research, medical technology, telecommunications, and intellectual property.

Building on the established reputation and credibility of the Institute for Policy Innovation, we have created the Center for Technology Freedom to explain to the American people and policy makers the policy challenges posed by technological changes and the economy. We also want to point the way for a society that will encourage free markets, free minds and free people.

We believe in a hands-on approach, working with industry to identify the real issues, in an effort to ultimately produce useful and directed studies, analysis and commentary. When we undertake a new initiative we enter into an intensive research and discovery phase which includes visiting with industry leaders, technical experts and policy leaders. Only after gaining this insight into the issues and an understanding of the complexity of the issue do we continue. We then engage in the actual study or analysis, culminating in a publication.

Basically, I started handling technology policy issues in 1995, before it was hip to be involved in tech issues. That is what provided me with my chance—no one wanted to handle those issues. Well, I guess it is true that bedfellows are strange in politics. Nevertheless, it is my honor to appear before this subcommittee to offer any insight or advice that I can.

I have to say that I do wish that the members of this subcommittee had been my law school professors. As I understand it, the legislation that we are here to examine has already been passed on to the full committee. How nice that would have been—to have a professor go ahead and give me an acceptable grade before they even studied the paper.

OVERVIEW

In the last decade we have watched as gambling has rolled across America. I grew up in Illinois and lived several years in Missouri and both of those states now allow gambling. The expansion never seems to end—first travelling riverboats, then boats that never had to move, then boats in a large pool of water or "boat in a moat", then what anyone would call a building still surrounded by that moat, then simply land based casinos. Apparently, the Internet gambling market is expanding rapidly as well. One estimate indicates that 43 million Internet gamblers will generate $2.3 billion in revenue by 2001. Obviously, the worldwide appetite for Internet gaming is great.

I do think we need to place this is some context however. Many would lead us to believe that every time someone boots up their computer or turns on WebTV that they are ready with credit card in hand and a risky spirit in their heart. In fact, nothing could be further from the truth. According to the Wall Street Journal, just this last December, only 2% of Internet users indicated that they go online at least once a month to gamble. That compares to 6% to trade stock, 17% to get investment advice, 22% to view pornography, 51% to read the daily news, 72% for research on services or products, or 96% to use e-mail.

This is likely a good time to provide my view on gambling in general—I think that it is, frankly, a tax on those who can't do math. That is not my original quote but to tell you the truth I don't recall who said it first.

I simply do not believe that unrestricted access to gambling is a healthy prospect or some symbol of evolution of personal freedom. I do, however, believe that this alternative is better than a federal power grab, or better than a government sponsored balkanization of the Internet. Perhaps though, a rational approach that regulates gambling, instead of the Internet, is the best of all.

The prospect of children gambling away in darkened rooms across the countryside is a frightening and popular image to conjure up. Fortunately, I believe that individuals are better than to let that scare story become a reality. I believe that individuals, not a central government are best suited to the task of averting this disaster.

I also believe that our federal government should be limited in size and scope, just as the Bill of Rights explicitly demands. In fact, the Internet has succeeded precisely because of the minimal legislative and regulatory controls. I believe that if the federal government begins to oppressively regulate the Internet, the temptation will be overwhelming in all cases of Internet issues. That approach will lead to the end of what the Internet could have become.

We must always defend the principle of federalism, and once you stand on principle then the worst that can be said of you is that you are principled.

I also want to add that I have long admired Congressman Goodlatte and his staff. His understanding and leadership regarding issues of the Internet, indeed all technology, and public policy should serve as an example to his colleagues. I have worked closely with his office in several circumstances but most proudly on the issue of encryption. I enjoy his insights and his hard work on behalf of Virginia and the nation. However, in this case I believe that some work must be done before a hasty decision is made.

I have absolutely no doubt as to the good intentions of those who support Internet gaming prohibition legislation, but their attempt will ultimately fail. The failure may not happen politically, in fact, I imagine that some sort of law will result. After all, we all know how those omnibus appropriations bills get loaded up with legislative initiatives that could not have passed muster in the full light of debate. But this legislation would certainly fail when attempting to actually prohibit Internet gambling, in other words, to actually work. The fundamental operating truths of the cyber-world are simply not being recognized. Whether we like it or not, unless an activity is globally abhorred, it is impossible to banish it from the World Wide Web, and even then only banished to the extent that we can and do enforce those laws.

PROHIBITION WITHOUT ENFORCEMENT

One of the true, as of yet unrealized, promises of the Internet is that geography becomes irrelevant—unfortunately congress has continued in trying to end that promise. Passing legislation before a critical analysis of issues such as nexus could be disastrous not just in this legislation but in all legislation related to the Internet.

In fact, the legislation is full of implications for nexus. A casual review demonstrates that in regards to Indian lands that the term "on" is used. Clearly a nexus issue. In addition, the very definitions are rife with decisions regarding nexus, such as a person buying a lottery ticket must physically be in the state for the lottery of which he will partake. So, in this case, the federal government has determined that the place of the buyer is the state with nexus. The implications for Internet tax are enormous.

We should also consider words such as "receiving" as in receiving a bet or wager. Where is the bet or wager received? At the server or at the personal computer? Should it matter? We are living in a world that no longer needs to cling to a definition of place as defined by geography. A conscious decision may be made to govern federal affairs by geography, but understand that this should be a conscious decision made with an understanding of the broad implications. Also, one should understand that this decision stands in opposition to the very nature of the Internet. To not answer this question fully and understand its implications is to let the issue of enforcement go unresolved.

Ironically, a decision on the nexus issue here easily leads to a decision regarding Internet taxation, a result I am certain many of us would like to avoid. What certainly seems clear from economic and regulatory history is that once a market is subject to the smallest regulation, it is only a matter of time until other forms of government intervention follow. That point needs to be made very clear—this legislation is not a regulation of an activity but a regulation of the Internet itself.

Not many years ago the on-line service providers fought valiantly against an attempt to hold them liable for the illegal use of copyright protected material being sent across their systems. They fought not just to avoid an unjust shifting in responsibility in the case of copyright, but also to avoid a wholesale shift in liability for any illegal activities. That same foresight should be applied in this case, and by this committee. What you do here, regarding Internet gaming, and both good and bad, will have impact in all other areas of Internet law.

A case in point, the French government recently learned a hard lesson about control of the Internet. The French enacted a poorly crafted and ineffective law intended to enhance their enforcement of Internet copyright law. However, failing to recognize the international character of the Internet, the French law backfired. The result was pirated materials appearing on Web sites around the world. Unfortunately, the U.S. Congress is headed toward the same sort of ineffective policy.

Did you know that nearly fifty countries now license and regulate Internet gaming? This alone makes it a safe bet that this legislation will not be able to effectively prohibit Americans from placing a bet on, let's say, the St. Louis Rams by email.

Why should this matter? I cannot find anywhere in the legislation any attempt to deal with operators who are beyond the reach of U.S. law enforcement. Without some way to reach these operators you will never stop a Web site from having gambling information, advertising or the games themselves available. My understanding is that no one has yet been able to answer this question, so from a very practical point of view I ask, why not spend time trying to answer that question than spending it trying to implement faulty policy?

Moreover, the legislation in no way seeks to limit demand. The gaming site operators are at risk but not the person who is gambling, and risking his or her family by "clicking the mouse and betting the house." Hence, this prohibition will never be as effective as the international efforts against child pornography. One basic question to ask is whether a supply approach will work on the Internet. Perhaps we would be better served by attacking the demand.

The French case clearly provides a perfect example of legislating without regard for enforcement, and hence without regard for the rule of law. Of course, we cannot as a society, allow advancements in technology to overrun the ability to govern. But ineffective legislation does nothing more than contribute to lawlessness. If citizens feel it is appropriate to break a law—merely because it is unenforceable—we ultimately weaken the underpinnings of our society with respect to all crimes, regardless of seriousness.

Just ask some of the governors about this thought when it comes to Internet taxation. All those years of allowing the use tax to go uncollected, largely, as they argue, because it is unenforceable, has left the impression with a great many of us that we do not owe a tax on remote purchases. Bad law plus no enforcement equates to no law.

PROHIBITION WITH THE WRONG ENFORCEMENT

The bill does not make placing a bet a federal crime. So how does this legislation attempt to enforce the ban? It would deputize online service providers (OSPs). After notification by law enforcement, OSPs would be required to deny access to web pages. This forces operators to change web addresses—a process that takes less than a minute. That point needs to be clear, that taking down a site does nothing but cause inconvience to an operator. This is not the analog world where you have to pack up and move to a new building. Unfortunately the answer is not that easy.

The real trouble is that this legislation treats Internet access as a government-granted privilege; the federal government wants to decide who can access the Web and under what conditions. This is regulation of the Internet not just an attempt to eliminate a certain undesired behavior.

Regardless of the OSP provision, the Justice Department will not be able to reach sites operating in foreign countries—especially those operating with the blessing of foreign governments that license their activities. So, prosecutors, at best, could be left pursuing individual gamblers who may have bet lunch on the outcome of the next Dallas Stars game. The bottom line—law enforcement will now chase bettors instead of drug dealers, gamblers instead of kidnappers.

PROHIBITION WITHOUT PRINCIPLE

For every member of congress and every citizen, the legislation should be very troubling. The bill broadens the scope of government sanctioned gaming. "Closed loop subscriber-based services" gambling for horse and dog races, as well as jai alai, would be given a nod of approval by the federal government for the potential of in-home gambling. Lotteries and hotel-casinos are also excepted from the Internet Gambling Prohibition Act and thereby seemingly are given some sort of legitimacy by our nation's government. Given the realities of the Internet and the language of this legislation what you end up with is a law that liberalizes gambling. Essentially, this legislation creates the impression of legality, but for state law to the contrary.

I have read the floor statements in both the House and Senate touting the need for a federal government ban on Internet gaming, or any federal action at all. Everything I have seen emphasizes the importance of protecting the country from rampant gambling. Okay, I can understand those sentiments. What I cannot understand is how the legislation even begins to measure up. The multiple carve outs for special interests make a mockery of the legislation in the first place, and make the prospect of prohibiting Internet gaming more impossible than an absolute ban.

I am baffled at how the federal government on the one hand is saying that gambling is eroding our values, placing our children at risk, and fostering addiction; but then, in the same legislation, says that as long as only certain gambling occurs or in this particular way then we are okay. Surely I am missing a point. Either gaming is okay and we merely want to serve the special interests by protecting the analog world, or gambling is indeed harmful, in which case this legislation should be titled the, "All Gambling Prohibition Act," and actually prohibit gambling. Well, maybe what we are saying is that the Devil is okay in small amounts, and as long as he doesn't hop on his laptop.

Greatly problematic from an Internet operations standpoint is the prohibition on on-line advertising. This, in simple terms, is called regulation of Internet content. This is not new to Congress. Legislation passed congress that attempted to regulate content, by means of an absolute ban. Those attempts were found to be unconstitutional and struck down. Putting aside the legal issues at hand, how do you really expect this to work? How do we propose to stop a foreign operated site that advertises gambling, and maybe even offers on-line gambling?

What happens if the advertising is on a radio station in Europe or in the Caribbean that may be listened to via the Internet? Are travel web-sites that offer vacation packages to jurisdictions where gaming is legal now going to be legal in a jurisdiction where gaming is illegal? For Web sites hosted in the United States you may have some luck with that approach, but what about internationally? Interestingly, I hear advertisements for casinos all the time in Dallas, where gambling is not legal, for casinos in Louisiana, where gambling is allowed—why would we treat the Internet differently? In fact, we should not treat the Internet differently, although I understand that temptation to do so.

The simple answer is that you cannot selectively winnow content from the Internet with federal legislation. Now, some elected officials have vowed to pull the plug on lines that "bring in" objectionable content. Okay, well there you have me—federal legislation could stop the content. We could set about creating a tele-Internet communications isolationist country. For that matter this entire approach assumes that some purveyor is sending material into the U.S. or into any particular state. That notion is entirely backward.

The Internet is a creation that in its original design was developed to survive a nuclear war—I guess meaning that the Web could be operated by the cockroaches that would survive. Nevertheless, you need to consider that fact very carefully as you try to partition off sections of the Internet. How is legislation going to do it? That question has never been answered and in fact, cannot be, because there is no solution that allows the Internet to continue to operate as it does and quash specific content.

How about a real world example—who favors child pornography except the horrid criminals that peddle their evil wares? What government allows it to flourish? No one. However it still exists, and even with making the supply and demand a criminal action. Okay, now take other pornography—let's say in a jurisdiction that outlaws supply. You think that it cannot be viewed on the Internet in those places? Remember that individuals go on-line eleven times more often to view pornography than to gamble. A much bigger issue to resolve and still not an effective solution.

This legislation will be just as porous—no restriction on demand, and many foreign governments looking to protect their growth industries. If we really are opposed to Internet gaming why not make the demand criminal conduct as well. The model of attacking supply and demand for products that we find objectionable may be past, unless those actions are universally abhorred. The way to solve this problem is to attack the demand side of the equation.

In fact, if we just stop a moment and consider how things really work the system is not so hard to understand. We can use your Congressional web-sites as a good example. Now I am sure that many of you have sites available for your constituents. Those sites do not go out to people; individuals go to those sites. To be absolutely precise individuals direct their computer to search out a particular web-site; they direct their computer to the server (a powerful computer), which holds the information for which they are searching. They then view the information on their computer that has collected the information sent in data packets to their location.

The bottom line is that the information would not have gotten to their computer but for their wanting it to be there. To say otherwise is to say that you actually want those telemarketing calls during dinner.

By permitting some types of gambling despite the "prohibition," the bill is a federal endorsement of gambling expansion. At the same time enforcement is absolutely impossible given the technological realities of the Internet. For gambling opponents, one has to balance the greater evil—the uncertainty surrounding wagering via the Net or the government affirmatively endorsing betting on the Kentucky Derby.

THE INDIVIDUAL STATES LOSE—AGAIN

I have always found as instructive reading a person's words very carefully and often not for what is said, but for what is not said. Take a look at the statements regarding federalism and Internet gaming prohibition legislation. The comments point out a list of items that are not pre-empted at the state level but utterly ignores the fact that if a state found it appropriate to allow gambling in the Internet that it would not be allowed to do so. Why not?

We are well aware that Internet gambling will continue. Right now nearly fifty countries allow and regulate Internet gambling. Again, even with the most basic understanding of the Internet we can appreciate that web sites will be available for viewing and interaction in the United States. So, why would the federal government wish to take away more states rights? Perhaps Bob Dole was the last Member of Congress to carry the 10th amendment with him.

This is not just a hypothetical issue. The state of Minnesota is creating a commission to look at the benefits of licensing Internet gaming operations. Under the current legislation, the state of Minnesota loses all its Constitutional rights regarding this issue. This legislation clearly goes beyond interstate issues and does, in fact, regulate intrastate activities.

BETTER SOLUTIONS?

Encryption has been pointed out as a means for solving another content debate. Mr. Goodlatte among others pointed out that in a world of robust encryption we could protect children and others from viewing pornographic material. Has anyone thought about whether encryption could be applied here to slip this Gordian Knot?

Why not require Internet gambling houses and bettors to exchange encryption passwords along with verification of the location of the bettor? Maybe the bettor could only make a wager from a particular location. Then, law enforcement has the ability to go to one location for the collection of information. Internet gaming operations, instead of the federal government bear the burden of figuring out a verification system for their members while gamers operate in a world of assurance. At the same time, the Internet is not limited by greater federal intrusion, and the rest of us are free from increasing arbitrary and ineffective government intrusion.

Perhaps this idea has been examined and found lacking, perhaps it has not been viewed at all. What I do know is that the fever to race legislation into law in the last Congress led to a lack of concern as to the effects that bad law would have along the way, for the Internet and the rule of law.

Another thought is to pass the digital signature legislation that is now being hung up in conference committee. In that legislation the government is not once again regulating lives and stripping states of rights, but instead it empowers individuals. Briefly, the legislation allows for complete electronic contracting, end-to-end electronic transactions. This is enabled, in part, by being able to absolutely identify the person at the other end of the transaction—an element I am sure we all remember from first year contracts. This simple solution applies easily here and answers every one of your arguments. If an operator knows whom the person is, their age, their place of residence and their current location, then what is left? With this we have no kids gambling, states can regulate as they see fit, not as Washington D.C. finds politically expedient, and limits can easily be placed on how much could be bet.

How about instead of using all the time trying to push ineffective federal actions and instead use this year educating the public on this issue. Everyone who favors this legislation should spend their time promoting your view of Internet gambling so that individuals will purchase filters to screen out gambling sites. The companies and organizations that back this measure could facilitate advertisements and fund the education. Imagine the real change you could be responsible for if everyone knew that in their homes they could eliminate the threat of gambling without the federal government spending one penny or passing one new law.

This effort along with the federal laws on the books, and the state laws, would produce far better results than believing that international gaming operators will be stopped. We would all be much better off by this attempt. No heavy handed federal involvement or regulation of the Internet, and a limitation on gambling that bubbles up from the grassroots—the real way to change attitudes in this country.

Of course, none of these ideas may be the best answer. Keep in mind that many other issues will require absolute identification, such as on-line voting. The federal government is now allowing for census forms to be completed on-line. If the federal government can accept that we can place on the Internet a census form and be confident that the submission is coming from an identifiable person, in a certain location, then why can't this committee, and this Congress, be satisfied in this case?

Again I urge that you re-think the position that more legislation is the answer when in fact the laws on the books may adequately cover what is needed, and if not, surely greater federal heavy handedness is not the answer.

CONCLUSION

Internet gambling is the canary in the coalmine. Once politicians regulate it, nothing will stop them from taxing and regulating other activities—merely because they can. If the legislation that you have before you passes, we will know that the prospect of a regulation-free Internet was too great of a threat to those who feel the need to exercise unrestrained federal government control. Passage will demonstrate that regardless of the topic, special interests like the horse and dog tracks will be able to exempt themselves in the chaos of legislative drafting. If this is truly the case, too bad for the Internet, too bad for the rule of law, and too bad for those opposed to gaming as a matter of principle.

Attachments:

Census Goes Online But Gets Few Hits
By D'Vera Cohn
Washington Post Staff Writer
Saturday, March 4, 2000; Page A10

The 2000 Census arrived in cyberspace yesterday, but only a few took advantage of the first-time opportunity to fill out their questionnaires over the Internet.

People can file electronically on the Census Web site (www.census.gov) by entering a 22-digit number printed on the form they receive, which also serves as their password. Five in six households receive the short form, which lets them respond via the Internet, but Census officials expect only a fraction to do so.

Census officials say they expect fewer than 8 million households, out of an estimated 120 million, to file electronically. But since most people will not receive their forms until later this month, officials were not surprised that only 11 forms were sent over the Internet by mid-afternoon yesterday. John Thompson, associate Census director, said no problems were reported with the site.

Census officials are not promoting the Internet for this count because their current operations are designed mainly for mail-in responses, and their outreach is targeted at people who are reluctant to file, which includes poorer people without computers.

Thompson said the use of the Internet this year is intended to be a learning experience.

"It's an emerging technology, and we want to learn about it," he said. This year, he said, "While we are using the Census to get experience in using the Internet . . . we wouldn't want to make the Internet our main vehicle for response."

Diane Harlow, of Warrenton, said she was thrilled to be one of the first to file via the Internet yesterday.

But as a U.S. Postal Service clerk, she felt a little guilty about Diverting business from her employer.

"It was a cinch," she said. "It was perfect. It was so simple. . . . If people want to do something exciting, it's a good way to do it."

Because she filed the short form, which does not ask about income or other more confidential information, Harlow said, she had few concerns about privacy. But she is "not brave enough to send my taxes over the Internet."

To assure security, the site will accept only one Census form for each password, Thompson said, and will not let people view their responses after they have submitted them.

Census officials suggest that people who file on the Internet ensure their browser employs 128-bit encryption, the security standard required for many business transactions over the Web.

The Census Bureau is not the first federal agency to allow electronic filing—the Internal Revenue Service got there first. But Census often has pioneered use of technology, such as being first with punch-card tabulation equipment, then computers, then mapping software.

Census officials say the Internet option will expand in future counts, but they almost did not allow it for this one.

"We didn't want it to be an embarrassment and we didn't want it to be insecure," Thompson said. "We believe we've solved those two problems."

Politics
Sit Down, Sign On, and Send Ballot
By Ben White
Washington Post
Sunday, March 5, 2000; Page A19

Americans have managed to do a remarkable number of things over the Internet—buy cars, book vacations, find spouses. One thing they haven't been able to do, however, is cast a meaningful ballot. That is about to change.

Next Saturday, Arizona Democrats plan to complete the first-ever binding online vote as part of their presidential nominating caucuses. Attorney General Janet Reno recently approved the plan that will allow Arizona Democrats to vote via the party Web site any time between Tuesday and Friday.

The party plans to install computers for Internet voting at 125 polling places. Reno cautioned that the Justice Department intends to monitor the voting closely to make sure it does not amount to discrimination against minorities and the poor, who are less likely to have Internet access at home.

That concern is also the subject of a lawsuit filed against the Arizona Democratic Party by a Virginia-based nonprofit group. A federal judge refused to halt the voting last week, denying a request for a temporary restraining order. But U.S. District Judge Paul Rosenblatt did not dismiss the case, and said the results might have to be set aside if the plaintiffs can prove that the voting amounted to discrimination.

H.F No. 3876, as introduced: 81st Legislative Session (1999–2000)
Posted on Feb 24, 2000

A bill for an act
relating to Internet gambling; requiring study of

costs and benefits.

BE IT ENACTED BY THE LEGISLATURE OF THE STATE OF MINNESOTA:

Section 1. [INTERNET GAMBLING STUDY.]

The house research office, Minnesota lottery research division, and office of senate counsel and research shall conduct a study of gambling on the Internet and shall issue a report on this matter by February 1, 2000. The study shall consider the benefits and costs to Minnesota from legalization of Internet gambling businesses operated within Minnesota, which conduct gambling for persons not resident in Minnesota. The study shall consider the financial impact on employment, potential costs and benefits to existing gambling industries, and impacts on potential gamblers. The departments of revenue and public safety, Minnesota planning, the lawful gambling control board, and the attorney general shall cooperate with this study.

Mr. CHABOT. I know that some of the members of the panel have flights out of here by 6:00, so, at least I can speak personally, I will try to keep my questions within 5 minutes.

I will begin with Mr. Minnix. Mr. Minnix, is it your view that it would be helpful to our education efforts, important to our universities and colleges, to have Congress pass legislation that sends a clear message that Internet gambling is an illegal activity?

Mr. MINNIX. Yes, quite definitely. We need to send a clear message that I do not think is present today. In my testimony, I mentioned all the advertising that is going on and these advertisings are costing these people a half-million to a million dollars to get that message out there. As far as our students and student athletes are concerned, this is legal because nobody is telling them otherwise. There is no clear message to them that this is an illegal activity. I think a law would be very helpful in protecting our young people in terms of giving them some idea as far as clarity exactly what is legal, what is illegal.

I would also add that that would also be a deterrent in terms of if any of these big multinational corporations get involved in this, at least they know what they can and cannot do.

Mr. CHABOT. Thank you. Mr. Whyte, you mentioned charities briefly in your testimony. Charitable organizations are presently permitted under Federal law and most State laws to conduct bingos and lotteries and similar games of chance provided that all the proceeds are dedicated to charitable purposes. I understand that some charitable organizations would like an exemption under this bill to conduct charitable gaming online. Would you have an opinion as to whether charitable gaming should be specifically included among the exemptions in this bill?

Mr. WHYTE. Charitable gaming is simply another form of gambling. We are neutral on gambling. For the National Council on Problem Gambling, it is irrelevant who is operating the game, whether it is commercial bingo, whether it is charitable bingo, Indian bingo. It is the gambling. We are neutral on the form. It is irrelevant.

Our other concern with charitable gambling is simply that most States permit any age. Some States, in fact, have no age limit whatsoever for charitable gambling. But specifically with this bill, we would not take a position on whether they should have the same rights as other forms. It would be the type of gambling.

Mr. CHABOT. Thank you. Mr. Walters, what would be the effect of an Internet gambling bill that fails to exempt State-regulated parimutuel industries?

Mr. WALTERS. I think quite definitely, Mr. Chairman, that it certainly would kill horse racing and greyhound racing in Oregon and I think in most States. The way this bill is phrased concerning computer interactive systems and that type of definition, it clearly would apply to the interstate simulcasting that has been the backbone of this industry for many years.

As I said in my testimony, I believe 75 to 80 percent of all of the wagering on horse and greyhound racing in today's modern world, where there is a lot of competition for the entertainment dollar, is through simulcasting, and the way that happens is there is a commingling of mutual pools. A race held in California. Bets are made at facilities around the country and it is all commingled in one pool at the race track in California. So if this bill did not contain these provisions—Senator Kyl does not want to call them exceptions, so I will refer to them as provisions—I think it quite definitely would kill legal horse and greyhound racing in this country.

Mr. CHABOT. Thank you. Let me come back to you, Mr. Whyte. Are regulated gambling operators more responsive to problem gambling concerns than unregulated?

Mr. WHYTE. Absolutely. As, in fact, Mr. Walters has said, the Oregon Racing Commission, I understand, has an extensive set of procedures and it has been our absolute experience that States with regulated gaming are much more responsive because there is an enforcement provision and there are regulators that we can go to.

Mr. CHABOT. My final question, Mr. Cleland, as you testified in your statement, it implied that this legislation was somehow an unreasonable burden on the Internet. Are you aware that less than a year ago, America Online, the Commercial Internet Exchange, the United States Telephone Association, and U.S. West wrote Senator Kyl thanking him for "adapting the bill to the technological realities and challenges of the Internet" and congratulating him for his work on virtually identical provisions?

Mr. CLELAND. Absolutely. My understanding of that letter and from—I used to work for Senator Ashcroft's office and we worked on this issue then. The issue was the same. What they had resolved was the issue of who would be liable for the transmission of material across their backbones, for example. In other words, could you hold AOL liable if I transmitted—sent an e-mail to you, sir, that said, hey, let us bet on lunch and you said, yes, let us go ahead and do that. The question was, could law enforcement then go after AOL to be held responsible for that transaction, and they very accurately—Mr. Kyl did, and perhaps Mr. Goodlatte—said, no, we will not allow them to go after the carrier of that information, assuming if you could get it at all. So that is to what they were referring.

To what I am referring is much broader and, frankly, goes right to the enforcement question. Mr. Kyl has said on the record, he would be happy to pull the plug if this kind of activity cannot be stopped, and that is why I said, well, you have me there. You pull the plug on all of our Internet connections that run outside this country and you can stop it with this legislation. But for that, you cannot.

Mr. CHABOT. Thank you, and I thank all the witnesses. My time is expired and we will hear from Mr. Scott.

Mr. SCOTT. Thank you. Mr. Walters, if this bill passed and allowed a specific exemption for horse racing only for the connections to the off-track betting parlors and not in the homes, what effect would the passage of the bill have on horse racing in Oregon?

Mr. WALTERS. It would affect it rather seriously, Representative Scott, because——

Mr. SCOTT. In fact, let me ask it another way. Do you allow people to plug in from home to cast their bets right now?

Mr. WALTERS. Yes. Oregon does, and seven other States do. That is account wagering. It has been legal in New York for 30 years.

Mr. SCOTT. That answers the question. Mr. Cleland, you were, because of time constraints, you had to talk very fast.

Mr. CLELAND. Yes.

Mr. SCOTT. Can you slow down a little bit and explain to us what effect this legislation would have if you have in Iraq a business setup for wagering with a provider with an ISP that is controlled by entities in Iraq? How could we enforce a prohibition against Internet betting, particularly if there is no liability on the gambler himself?

Mr. CLELAND. I do not want to be overly flippant, but there is none. The only way you would be able to stop it is if you had—and the Department of Justice, frankly, said they cannot reach—there is no reach to a provider who is another country and that is what you would have to do, because the website will be hosted on a server. As information comes into the country, I am baffled as to how we could possibly stop information at point of entry into the country. If you take that——

Mr. SCOTT. Does point of entry into the country mean anything?

Mr. CLELAND. It does not mean anything to the Internet so far as I know. There are a lot of things that could mean something, but I have no idea to what Mr. Kyl was referring. Interestingly, if you could do that, then I think that is a greater argument for letting the States regulate themselves, because if the Internet could be stopped at an arbitrary political subdivision, then why not let the States stop it at their border and keep the Federal Government out of the Internet and out of our affairs.

Mr. SCOTT. But in this scenario that I mentioned, it would be totally unenforceable?

Mr. CLELAND. To the best of my knowledge.

Mr. SCOTT. Thank you, Mr. Chairman.

Mr. CHABOT. Thank you. The gentleman's time has expired and we will defer now to Mr. Goodlatte.

Mr. GOODLATTE. Thank you, Mr. Chairman. I want to take exception to that contention for a number of reasons. First of all, if someone is outside of the United States, it does not mean that if they enter the United States, they cannot be arrested and prosecuted, and many of these people are folks who will want to visit the United States.

Secondly, it does not preclude the United States from entering into cooperative agreements with foreign nations who violate our laws to extradite people into the United States.

Finally, it does not preclude the ability to enforce through the credit transaction that has to take place, because you cannot, as you can in a casino, put your $20 bill on the table. You have to go through some other entity to transmit those funds to the offending operator that is operating offshore in order to participate in gaming.

So I think there are lots of tools available to law enforcement to prosecute those who are at more remote locations, albeit certainly more difficult to do than somebody who might be in Minnesota or across the State line from Wisconsin.

Mr. CLELAND. Absolutely on all points. I think e had a scenario, some Iraqi site with, I am assuming, Iraqi owners. I was not sure— —

Mr. GOODLATTE. Does Visa transmit credit to sites in Iraq?

Mr. CLELAND. Oh, I am sorry. I was talking about the physical presence. I was not sure they are going to be real happy to come to the United States. On that point, I would say that today, that is true. In a world of digicash, which with any luck is within a year or two away, I am not sure that that argument holds because you will have money, completely electronic flow where you are moving around electrons essentially from bank accounts where nothing physically is transacted.

Mr. GOODLATTE. Well, you are certainly moving around electrons, but whether or not the responsible banking authorities that make those transfers can cooperate with law enforcement as needed— —

Mr. CLELAND. Absolutely. If that happens, then you are right. We have greater reach. I would assume that under any legislation we would seek those kind of efforts. But that in no way addresses the notion that people can still sit in their bedrooms, still gamble online, and if a site is located in another country, at least from the Federal law, and I understand the State law point, that the States can still go after them, but from the Federal law standpoint, there is nothing that can happen in that transaction.

Mr. GOODLATTE. Let me ask you this, Mr. Cleland. There is also a very serious problem with child pornography on the Internet— —

Mr. CLELAND. Absolutely.

Mr. GOODLATTE The best description I heard of child pornography was viewing a crime in the process of being committed, when you are talking about children ten, 12, 13 years old engaged in sexual activities with other children or with adults and so on and there is a tremendous market of this on the Internet. Would you argue that we should not attempt, given the acknowledged difficulty of dealing with that problem, that we nonetheless should not in any way attempt to restrict child pornography as it proliferates on the Internet— —

Mr. CLELAND. Absolutely— —

Mr. GOODLATTE [continuing]. From Iraq or any other country in the world?

Mr. CLELAND. Absolutely, we should, and fortunately, I mentioned this actually in my testimony. I think it is very important to note that child pornography is universally abhorred and gives us a certain help in stopping those from spreading child pornography, and also— —

Mr. GOODLATTE. But since gambling is not, you are saying that the lowest common denominator should prevail, that if one community says they love gambling and the other community does not, that the other community is not within their rights to try to restrict it when it still has all of the same effects in that community regarding bankruptcies and crime and family problems and addiction and so on? All those problems exist in the community where that person lives, whether or not they are doing it online or whether they are doing it at a casino, and the community can clearly decide not to have the casino. Why should they not have the tools given to them to try to keep it from affecting their community if it is done on the Internet?

Mr. CLELAND. I completely agree with you. I would go ahead and ban all gambling. I say that right in my testimony. I think gambling is a tax on people who do not do math. [Laughter.]

So I am happy to have an absolute prohibition on gambling. I would encourage the committee to consider that rather than something that takes a hackneyed approach and does things, as we heard from virtually everyone up here who talked about the technological angle, enforcement ultimately is not possible in the way it has been described and, frankly, it creates differences in the way the law is going to be applied vis-a-vis the Wire Act.

Mr. GOODLATTE. Let me take exception with a comment in your testimony that the bill is not a regulation of an activity but a regulation of the Internet itself. It— —

Mr. CLELAND. It is.

Mr. GOODLATTE. Well let me take a second and ask you to define what you mean by that. When the Securities and Exchange Commission this week went after classic stock manipulators, a bunch of kids in law school at Georgetown, no less, who used their website to push up a stock price and then secretly dumped their shares, is that regulation of an activity or is that regulation of the Internet? Does it prove too much to say that anything that affects activity, in that case criminal activity, on the Internet amounts to regulation of the Internet?

Mr. CLELAND. No, absolutely not. That activity should be prohibited. On the other hand, we should not tell arbitrary political subdivisions what they—to pass a law, frankly that cannot be enforced— —

Mr. GOODLATTE. Most political subdivisions do not regard themselves as arbitrary. In fact, wars have been fought over the borders— —

Mr. CLELAND. Absolutely.

Mr. GOODLATTE [continuing]. That have created those subdivisions.

Mr. CLELAND. Sir, you probably know far better than I, given your position in the Internet caucus, that the Internet is completely blind to those political subdivisions, for better or for worse, and I am not going to take a position on either side of that— —

Mr. GOODLATTE. And I agree with that observation. In fact, in my opening statement, I made that same observation. But that does not mean that you have to abandon all means of recognized civilized activity because it is harder, given the prolific nature of the Internet and the way it easily crosses political jurisdictions. It still does not mean that you should not attempt to deal with those aspects of the Internet that society and a particular community views as harmful.

Mr. CLELAND. Absolutely, which is exactly why I said that when you bring into law laws that cannot be enforced and we know that ahead of time, you frankly destroy the rule of law in this country. That is exactly my point.

Mr. CHABOT. The gentleman's time has expired.

Mr. GOODLATTE. I thank the chairman.

Mr. CHABOT. Thank you very much, and I want to thank the panel for their testimony. I think all the panels this afternoon were excellent, and at this time, we are adjourned.

[Whereupon, at 5:23 p.m., the subcommittee was adjourned.]

APPENDIX

MATERIAL SUBMITTED FOR THE HEARING RECORD

NATIONAL FOOTBALL LEAGUE,
New York, NY, March 15, 2000.

Hon. WILLIAM MCCOLLUM, *Chairman,*
Subcommittee on Crime,
Committee on the Judiciary,
House of Representatives, Washington, DC.

DEAR CHAIRMAN MCCOLLUM: On behalf of the National Football League, I want to thank you for holding a hearing recently on H.R. 3125, the "Internet Gambling Prohibition Act of 1999", and to urge prompt adoption of this important legislation. This bill represents a balanced and effective response to the growing problem of gambling, including sports gambling, on the Internet. I ask that this letter be included in the record. I also want to address some matters that were raised at the hearing.

Why the NFL Supports the Internet Gambling Prohibition Act, H.R. 3125

For many years the NFL, along with other sports leagues, has aggressively protected the integrity of their games by adopting strict rules against gambling or any association with gambling. Put simply, gambling and sports don't mix. Gambling, or the possibility of gambling, can undermine the loyalty of fans and cheapen the outcomes of games. Gambling can distract players, coaches and referees. The unfortunate experience of college point-shaving scandals in recent years is a sober reminder to all involved with professional and amateur sports of the need to preserve the separation between sports and gambling.

In 1992, when some states threatened to institute a sports lottery, Congress passed the Professional and Amateur Sports Protection Act (PASPA), which prohibits state-sponsored sports gambling in all states except Nevada and, to a limited extent, Oregon. PASPA arrested the growth of government-sanctioned sports gambling. However, the Internet, with its worldwide reach, its ease of use, its relative anonymity, and its penetration into nearly every school, college dorm room, and home, could result in an explosion of sports gambling. The growing proliferation of off-shore Internet gambling Web sites is evidence that this issue is not merely theoretical. This phenomenon greatly concerns those responsible for maintaining the integrity of athletic contests. Congress must adopt legislation to ensure the latest technology does not shred existing federal and state gambling statutes. We must not permit Internet gambling to overwhelm the sound policy decision embodied in PASPA and prior legislation separating sports and gambling.

H.R. 3125 is a strong answer to the problem of Internet gambling for three reasons:

First, it establishes a workable and effective enforcement mechanism to stop or curb Internet gambling activity. Current law, with its emphasis on prosecution, simply is inadequate to require Internet providers to actually block access to Internet gambling sites, many of which are off-shore. The mechanism in H.R. 3125, which was carefully negotiated with AOL and other Internet service providers, would accomplish this goal without interfering with Internet operations.

Second, the bill clarifies that federal law prohibits a person engaged in a gambling business from using the Internet to make a bet or wager. At a time when the Internet gambling business is still being formed, this strong statement by the U.S. government now will have a powerful deterrent effect.

Third, because of the ubiquity of the Internet, any serious attempt to address this problem must occur at the national level. States simply cannot tackle this problem by themselves. In fact, that is why the National Association of Attorneys General

is one of the principal supporters of strong federal Internet gambling legislation, and has strongly endorsed the bill in both this House and in the Senate.

H.R. 3125 Has Effective Mechanisms To Reach Foreign Web Sites

One of the questions that arose from the hearing was whether the bill could be used to stop foreign Web sites from reaching U.S. customers. Ranking Member Scott, in a question to Assistant Attorney General DiGregory from the Department of Justice, asked what can be done about a foreign gambling site, and Mr. DiGregory responded that the Department would have difficulty prosecuting the foreign Web site operator. Though we defer to Mr. DiGregory on the reach of the prosecutorial powers of the Department, this answer misses a crucial feature—indeed, from our perspective, the most significant feature—of the bill: the ability to obtain a court order requiring a U.S.-based Internet Service Provider (ISP) to block access to a foreign gambling site. Thus, it does not matter whether the foreign site is in Iran, or Antigua or Australia—if law enforcement identifies the site and obtains a court order, then the ISP, consistent with the important provisions in the bill safeguarding the operations of the Internet, must block access to that foreign site. Nor should it be overlooked that this remedy—the critical one from our perspective—was carefully negotiated with the leading ISPs and is designed both to effectively limit gamble sites without compromising the operations of the Internet.

Another question that arose was whether the "cat-and-mouse" game of Web sites constantly changing their addresses could defeat the blocking mechanisms proposed in the bill. There are two reasons why this concern is misplaced. First, gambling sites that take on a "fly-by-night" character are unlikely to be able to attract customers willing to trust them with their bets. In this regard, online gambling is different from other Internet enterprises which operate in a stealth environment; to gain customers gambling businesses need to show that they are stable enough to be around to pay any winnings. Second, the Internet technology used to route traffic is constantly being upgraded and improved, and as a result, routing tables should be able to keep track of any rapid changes in address that do take place.

We greatly appreciate the hard work that you and your staff have put forth to advance this important legislation. We remain committed to assisting you in any way that we can to secure passage of this bill during this session of Congress.

We request that this letter be included in the record of the hearing.

Sincerely,

JEFFREY PASH, *Executive Vice President and General Counsel.*

cc: Subcommittee Members

○